Collector's Encyclopedia of Noritake

by
Joan Van Patten

COLLECTOR BOOKS
P.O. Box 3009
Paducah, KY 42001

Searching For A Publisher?

We are always looking for knowledgeable people considered to be experts within their fields. If you feel that there is a real need for a book on your collectible subject and have a large comprehensive collection, contact us.

COLLECTOR BOOKS
P.O. Box 3009
Paducah, Kentucky 42002-3009

Additional copies of this book may be ordered from:

COLLECTOR BOOKS
P.O. Box 3009
Paducah, Kentucky 42002-3009

@$19.95 Add $2.00 for postage and handling.

Copyright: Joan Van Patten, 1984
Values Updated, 1994

This book or any part thereof may not be reproduced without the written consent of the Author and Publisher.

Printed by IMAGE GRAPHICS, INC., Paducah, Kentucky

Dedication

Dedicated to my wonderful family and friends who helped make this book a reality.

My candle burns at both ends;
It will not last the night;
But, ah, my foes, and oh, my friends --
It gives a lovely sight.

Edna St. Vincent Millay

Acknowledgements

"Snowflakes are one of nature's most fragile things,
but just look at what they can do when they stick
together."

Vesta M. Kelly

And may I add, so too with Noritake collectors and lovers.

First, I would like to thank my publisher, Bill Schroeder, for having faith in this project and for always doing such a terrific job with my books. Also my thanks go to Steve Quertermous, my editor at Collector Books for all his help and support.

The majority of photos were taken by my sister-in-law, Marie Young. We have traveled to many cities and localities to gather all these wonderful pictures and I thank her for always being available when I needed her. Her enthusiasm for the project helped us pass many a tedious hour.

The Noritake Company has been most helpful to me in my search for information and I wish to take this opportunity to thank Mr. Yuki Kato in the New York office and T. Kaikawa in Japan for all the photos, backstamps and information that was mailed to me.

My good friends, Rita Gillis and Viola Breeves provided the majority of items which were photographed in the book. Marie and I spent several days at their homes on Long Island shooting pictures of these fantastic pieces. We were royally entertained by them and I appreciate all the work they went through in setting up all the items to be photographed. Without their help this book would never have become a realty.

My friend, Nancy Madigan, boxed up a number of her favorite Noritake items and mailed them on to me so that we could take photos. Many thanks Nancy, your help was appreciated.

Jean Cole allowed us to photograph several of her Noritake pieces and Berniece Gershon, Susan Garrison and Mary Falat sent me numerous photos to use. Thank you.

I also wish to thank Peggy Rousch for sending all the saucers that we photographed and also Clyde Stover for the photos of the Noritake Museum which he took on a recent trip.

Barbara Soper and the Buffalo Library have made an excellent contribution to the book with the information on the Larkin Company and I am grateful to be able to include it.

Others I wish to thank for photos and/or information are: Jess Berry, Robert Burich, Cathy Chudley, Gil Corriveau, Sharon Endejan, Sharlene Floam, Bernard and Fran Golden, Corrine Gould, Gary Graves, Larry Hartnell, Cindy Hoeper, Joyce Houran, Jim and Jane Keeton, Beulah Martinkus, Ruby May, George and Kathy Murphy, Max Munsey, Joan Oates and her husband Ken for the photos, Ben Perez, Bob Pierce, Lee Smith, Linda Van Orden, Keith and Gail Wilson, Kathy Wojciechowski, Fannie Young and Michael and Marie Young.

The price guide also took many, many hours to prepare and I would like to thank Viola Breves and Rita Gillis for the time they spent helping me with it.

As well as being a learning experience this book has also helped me make many new friends for which I am thankful. To both my old and new friends I say thank you from the bottom of my heart for all your help but mostly for your friendship and encouragement.

Contents
Noritake China, 1921-1941

Introduction

Noritake collecting is a lust that is never quenched,
but grows more inflamed and madder by enjoyment.
Adaptation of a quote by Thomas Otway.

Writing a book on Noritake collectibles, no matter how much information it may contain, is like trying to remove all the water from an ocean with a thimble. So many items were manufactured and imported into the United States that it would take numerous volumes to adequately cover the subject. Since that is not a realistic goal at this time perhaps we should merely consider this book as a starting point. Hopefully, it will whet the appetite of collectors and researchers and lead to new discoveries and information.

Noritake items are not antiques but their price range is beginning to suggest a title other than just collectibles. Collectiques is the term I have coined for these pieces. They're semi-antique and very collectible, everything all rolled into one.

Over the years most items seem to need a period of hibernation before they're fashionable again and the Noritake marked pieces from the 1921-41 period have been "sleepers" until now. Collectors and dealers are just beginning to appreciate these items and their value is starting to skyrocket as the supply dwindles. Age itself is not a virtue with collectibles but quality is what should determine value and desirability. The majority of these pieces fall into that category. It is true that now and then one will find some items that have not been as well painted as others, or there are those worn with time, or perhaps cracked, chipped, etc., but the collector must avoid these wares and stick to the pieces that will continue to grow in value because of their fine quality and workmanship.

It must be noted that Nippon and Japan are merely the designation of country of origin and many of the Noritake era pieces discussed in this book are identical to the Nippon marked ones. The only difference will be that the word Japan is found on the backstamp.

The Nippon era (1891-1921) for porcelain wares has been extensively covered in *The Collector's Encyclopedia of Nippon Porcelain, Series I and Series II* and collectors should refer to them for further background information. Hundreds of early Noritake pieces will be found in these two books. The so-called Noritake "collectiques" that most collectors refer to however, are those manufactured by the Noritake Co. during the years of 1921-41. Before this period the items fall into the "Nippon" category. After the bombing of Pearl Harbor in 1941 items from Japan were, of course, not imported into the United States. The Noritake Co. has advised me that the Noritake "Made in Occupied Japan" backstamp was not used by them until August 1947 when their export trade was reopened and this lasted until 1952 when the Japan-U.S. Peace Treaty was made. They continue in their correspondence to say "For the first two years it was applied to the Rose China backstamp." In 1946 and 1947 the Noritake Co. did not want to supply the U.S. Military personnel with items using the brand name of Noritake but instead named it "Rose China" since they did not have confidence that they would be able to produce the high quality of pre-war standards set for their wares due to the shortage of superior raw materials, equipment and skillful employees. The Noritake Co. did not want to spoil the high reputation that they had established in the pre-war days in the United States. They say that their records show that besides the Rose China backstamp one other backstamp* was applied to the wares with the words "Made in Occupied Japan", however it is clear that the backstamp was somehow misused and should not have been used before 1948. Then in 1948 they started to again use the "Noritake China M in wreath" on wares as better quality of materials became available and enabled them to manufacture the same high quality they had done before. The actual exportation of wares bearing this mark and the "Made in Occupied Japan" on it was made in the next year, 1949. Registrations of these three trademarks were made as mentioned below:

Rose China: 1950 in Japan.
Noritake with symbol, made in Occupied Japan: in 1949 in Japan and in 1950 in U.S.A.

Noritake China M in wreath made in Occupied Japan: in 1949 in Japan (The original trademark "Noritake China in wreath, Japan" started to be used in 1933 and was registered in the same year in Japan).

The "Occupied Japan" era is covered in several good books. In Gene Florence's definitive work on this subject *The Collector's Encyclopedia of Occupied Japan Collectibles* he says that "All items made in Japan, from the beginning of our occupation at the end of World War II until April 28, 1952, when the occupation ended, that were to be exported to the States had to be marked in one of four ways: "Japan", "Made in Japan", "Occupied Japan" or "Made in Occupied Japan"." And of course, many desirable items have been produced since then by the Noritake Co. as it is one of the most famous and prestigious companies in the world making fine china. These items are also collectible in their own right but generally when collectors are referring to Noritake "collectiques" they mean those manufactured during the years of 1921-41, the years I have chosen to cover in this book.

In October of 1890, the McKinley Tariff Act named for Rep. William McKinley who sponsored it, was passed by Congress. McKinley drafted this bill at the insistence of the Easterners in the United States who wanted more protection for United States manufacturers. The tariff act of the Fifty First Congress stated the following:

Chapter 1244, Section 6: "That on and after the first day of March, eighteen hundred and ninety-one, all articles of foreign manufacture, such as are usually or ordinarily marked, stamped, branded or labeled, and all packages containing such or other articles, shall, respectively, be plainly marked, stamped, branded or labeled in legible English words, so as to indicate the country of their origin, and unless so marked, stamped, branded or labeled they shall not be admitted to entry".

In March of 1921, the government reversed its position and decided that the word Nippon was a Japanese word, the English equivalent being Japan. Customs agents were then instructed that as of Sept. 1, 1921, merchandise from Japan, the marking of which is governed by this provision of law, should not be released when bearing only the Japanese word "Nippon" to indicate the country of origin. Thus the era of Nippon marked goods was over.

Collecting Noritake pieces can be both an educational and rewarding experience. It gives us the opportunity to learn about the items' history and how they were made. It's exciting, fascinating and addictive.

For one to have a truly great collection though, hard work is required but for most it's a labor of love. The best collections are carefully and lovingly gathered over the years and not formed by happenstance. Every collection is as unique as the collector who assembled it. Great collections are ruled by passion and not just reason. Don't be commonplace and cater to the tastes of the majority. Buy only those objects which personally appeal to you and buy the best you can afford. We express our individuality by collecting so BUY WHAT YOU LOVE!

A good collection also requires a considerable amount of self discipline and common sense. Shop carefully. Of course you're bound to make some mistakes but only by doing so can you learn from them and add to your storehouse of knowledge. Most collectors sell off their early mistakes and trade up to items of better quality.

Some people regard their collections as investments. Unlike certificates of deposit, stock, etc. their investment can be enjoyed daily and that enjoyment is like a free "dividend" of pleasure on their purchase.

These items will be your children's heirlooms and in generations to come, their children's. There is a pride and reward involved in successful collecting. There is also the exhileration of combing dusty corners of old barns and attics and rummaging through tables at flea markets and antique shows. There is the hope of finding a treasure, the excitement of buying something you love. The past seems to enrich the present. It shows us where we've been and where we're going.

Research your subject for collecting is enhanced by learning. You can reach your goals of having a "great" collection but it if often requires going out on a limb. But as the old saying goes "if you don't, you'll never get the fruit".

About Japan

Welcome to Japan, dozo Nihon-e oide kudasai, the crossroads of the East and West.

Japan is a nation of islands said by some to form the shape of a giant serpent. The coast is irregular producing a myriad of inlets, bays, coves and harbors. The islands total over 3,000 and are both large and small. They stretch in a long irregular half moon for 1,860 miles.

The total land area is a little smaller than that of California and the country boasts a population of over 116 million people in a land of which four-fifths is not arable. It is definitely a very densely populated nation.

At first glance Japan seems to be overwhelmingly westernized, however, the country's rich heritage still governs the everyday life of the people.

The climate varies from one end to the other, much like the United States. Kyushu can be compared to Florida, Hokkaido has snowy winters and the weather in Tokyo is much like that of Washington, D.C. Since less than one-fifth of the land is good for farming, fish is important to their diet and also as a major export.

It's a land of earthquakes and violent typhoons. It is also an island of mountains, many of which are volcanic. Because of these, thousands of hot springs are located in Japan. There are fast rivers and mountainous terrain. There are also the contrasts of rickshaws and monorails, modern apartment buildings and flimsy native houses made of bamboo and paper. No place is further than 90 miles to the open sea.

The four main islands which comprise about 98% of the total area are Honshu (the largest) which means Middle Kingdom or middle provinces or countries. The capital, Tokyo is located here. Hokkaido (the second largest) means northern seaway or road, Shikoku (third largest) means four provinces or countries, and Kyushu (the smallest) means nine provinces.

Mt. Fuji is its most spectacular mountain and reaches a height of 12,365 ft. The Japanese say this is easy to remember because there are 12 months in a year and 365 days in a year which equal 12,365.

Japan, also called Nippon, is referred to as "The Land Of The Rising Sun". Its floral name is "The Land of the Cherry Blossoms". In ancient times the Chinese called Japan "Zippon" which meant "Origin of the Sun" and they called their own country "Land of the Setting Sun".

Over the years the Japanese have borrowed from other cultures but have always adapted and altered in most cases to fit their needs.

During the Jomon period, estimated to have begun in 7,000 B.C., earthenware vessels were made. They were unglazed fired clay, decorated with cord markings and often garish in appearance. These all purpose clay pots were used for holding water, storage of food and even the burial of bones. Jo means cord or rope and mon means design or pattern, hence a cord marked pottery. These neolithic people fished and dug clams for food. Houses in Jomon times were built over open pits looking like a teepee but part was in the ground and part on top. They learned to eventually build without a center post so the fireplace could go in the center of the building where all could gather for warmth or cooking.

The Yayoi period dates from 400 B.C. to 400 A.D. The pottery of this time span was reddish gray and thinner than the Jomons. It was also fired at a higher temperature. More modest decoration is found on these wares.

From 400 A.D. to 600 A.D. gigantic tombs or so-called keyhole shaped sepulchral mounds were formed by the people. This "tomb period" is recognized by the organization of the people into series of clans, subdivided into guilds such as weavers, soldiers, actors, smiths, etc. Most of the tombs found are simple circular mounds of earth but some do have the unique keyhole design.

In 1638, in an attempt to isolate Japan from outside influences, the shogunate barred all ports to foreigners except the Dutch and the Chinese at Nagasaki. The Japanese proclamation stated that there would be no ship building and should someone succeed in getting out he would face death upon return and the same penalty applied to any foreigner who sought to enter. All through the 1800's Yankee captains tried to visit Japan but in vain. This period of isolation lasted until 1853.

On November 17, 1852, Commodore Matthew C. Perry left the United States to deliver a letter from President Fillmore. A few months before Fillmore left office he sent the letter with Perry expressing a wish that the two nations should "live in friendship" and "trade with each other". Since Japan was halfway around the world, by the time the letter was delivered he was no longer President.

The letter from President Fillmore to The Emperor of Japan went as follows:

"Great and Good Friend! I send you this public letter by Commodore Matthew C. Perry, an officer of the highest rank in the Navy of the United States, and commander of the squadron now visiting your Imperial majesty's dominions.

"I have directed Commodore Perry to assure your Imperial Majesty that I entertain the kindest feelings towards your Majesty's person and government; and that I have no other object in sending him to Japan, but to propose to your Imperial Majesty that the United States and Japan should live in friendship, and have commercial intercourse with each other.

"The constitution and laws of the United States forbid all interference with the religious or political concerns of other nations. I have particularly charged Commodore Perry to abstain from every act which could possibly disturb the tranquility of your Imperial Majesty's dominions.

"The United States of America reach from ocean to ocean, and our territory of Oregon and state of California lie directly opposite to the dominions of your Imperial Majesty. Our steam-ships can go from California to Japan in eighteen days.

"Our great state of California produces about sixty millions of dollars in gold, every year, besides silver, quicksilver, precious stones, and many other valuable articles. Japan is also a rich and fertile country, and produces many very valuable articles. Your Imperial Majesty's subjects are skilled in many of the arts. I am desirous that our two countries should trade with each other, for the benefit both of Japan and the United States.

"We know that the ancient laws of your Imperial Majesty's government do not allow of foreign trade except with the Dutch. But as the state of the world changes and new governments are formed, it seems to be wise from time to time to make new laws. There was a time when the ancient laws of your Imperial Majesty's government were first made.

"About the same time, America, which is sometimes called the New World, was first discovered and settled by the Europeans. For a long time there were but a few people, and they were poor. They have now become quite numerous; their commerce is very extensive; and they think that if your Imperial Majesty were so far to change the ancient laws as to allow a free trade between the two countries, it would be extremely beneficial to both.

"If your Imperial Majesty is not satisfied that it would be safe, altogether, to abrogate the ancient laws which forbid foreign trade, they might be suspended for five or ten years, so as to try the experiment. If it does not prove as beneficial as was hoped, the ancient laws can be restored. The United States often limit their treaties with foreign states to a few years, and then renew them or not, as they please.

"I have directed Commodore Perry to mention another thing to your Imperial Majesty. Many of our ships pass every year from California to China; and great numbers of our people pursue the whale fishery near the shores of Japan. It sometimes happens in stormy weather that one of our ships is wrecked on your Imperial Majesty's shores. In all such cases we ask and expect, that our unfortunate people should be treated with kindness, and that their property, should be protected, till we can send a vessel and bring them away. We are very much earnest in this.

"Commodore Perry is also directed by me to represent to your Imperial Majesty that we understand there is a great abundance of coal and provisions in the empire of Japan. Our steam-ships, in crossing the great ocean, burn a great deal of coal, and it is not convenient to bring it all the way from America. We wish that our steam-ships and other vessels should be allowed to stop in Japan and supply themselves with coal, provisions and water. They will pay for them, in money, or anything else your Imperial Majesty's subjects may prefer; and we request your Imperial Majesty to appoint a convenient port in the southern part of the empire, where our vessels may stop for this purpose. We are very desirous of this.

"These are the only objects for which I have sent Commodore Perry with a powerful squadron to pay a visit to your Imperial Majesty's renowned city of Yedo; friendship, commerce, a supply of coal, and provisions and protection for our shipwrecked people.

"We have directed Commodore Perry to beg your Imperial Majesty's acceptance of a few presents. They are of no great value in themselves, but some of them may serve as specimens of the articles manufactured in the United States, and they are intended as tokens of our sincere and respectful friendship.

"May the Almighty have your Imperial Majesty in his great and holy keeping!

"In witness whereof I have caused the great seal of the United States to be hereunto affixed, and have subscribed the same with my name, at the city of Washington in America, the seat of my government, on the thirteenth day of the month of November, in the year one thousand eight hundred and fifty-two.

Your Good Friend,
Millard Fillmore"

President Fillmore's letter was encased in a beautiful rosewood box, written on vellum and sealed with gold.

Perry left on the *Mississippi* which was the first operated steam vessel in the Navy. After anchoring in Hong Kong on April sixth in 1853, he was joined by several other ships and departed for Japan on May 23rd. The journey took three days before the four ships entered the harbor of Naha at Okinawa.

On July 14th the letter was given to the Prince of Idzu and the Prince of Iwami for delivery to the Emperor.

On July 17th the four ships sailed away promising to return for an answer. On February 25th, 1854 Perry returned dropping anchor off Kanagawa. Finally on March 31st of '54 the Treaty of Kanagawa was formally signed. This provided for the appointment of an American Consul to reside in Shimoda, the ports of Hakodate and Shimoda were opened for trade and the assured safe refuge for Americans cast upon Japanese shores was promised.

Perry arrived home on January 12, 1855. President Pierce influenced the Senate to ratify the trade treaty with Japan. Townsend Harris was appointed the first American Consul at Shimoda and proved to be a very competent diplomat. Perry's expedition opened the doors of Japan and awakened the dormant country. In 1868 a new constitutional government was formed in Tokyo and Japan set out a course of rapid modernization.

Since this time the Japanese have been encouraged to adopt Western technology and industrialization. Japan had once been an agricultural country but since the doors were opened to Western influences it is now one of the most modern nations in the world.

9

History of the Morimura Brothers

History of the Morimura Bros., forerunner of the Noritake Company reprinted with permission of Morimura Bros., Inc. and Noritake Co. Limited.

Aspiring to National Prosperity through Foreign Trade

Our company was born a full century ago when Morimura Gumi, a forerunner, was founded in 1876. This was during the Meiji era—the so-called era of enlightment and civilization. More precisely, it was conceived 18 years earlier in 1859, when young Ichizaemon Morimura, sixth generation head of the Morimura family, was awakened to the currents of the time and made up his fertile mind to expand Japan's foreign trade.

After nearly 300 years of isolationism, the Tokugawa Shogunate decided to open Japan's doors to the world. Two years later in 1860, an envoy was dispatched to the United States to ratify the Treaty of Commerce and Navigation between the two countries.

Ichizaemon Morimura VI was assigned the task of providing the envoy with gifts and foreign monies. While carrying out this important assignment, he discovered that the monetary exchange rate was extremely unfavorable to Japan and feared that unilateral trade with resultant losses from such unfavorable exchange rate, if unremedied, would have a highly adverse effect on the future of Japan.

He consulted Professor Yukichi Fukuzawa, his friend and founder of Keio Gijyuku University, and Professor Fukuzawa immediately advised, "There is no alternative but to increase exportation and thus get the money back to save the country."

Awakened to the importance of foreign trade, Ichizaemon firmly resolved to dedicate his life to the realization of national prosperity on the basis of foreign trade. This was in the spring of 1860 when Ichizaemon, called Ichitaro as a child, was 22-years-old.

Founding of Morimura Gumi

In May 1866 the Shogunate took a bold step and permitted overseas travel in order to promote education and trade. From this development, Ichizaemon judged that the chance for expanding foreign trade was drawing near and sent his younger brother, Yutaka, to study in Keio Gijyuku under the tutelage of Professor Fukuzawa, anticipating that he would become a future collaborator in fulfilling his ambition.

In an effort to meet his elder brother's expectations, Yutaka vigorously applied himself to his studies. He graduated with an outstanding academic record and later became an associate professor in his alma mater.

More than two years went by before the chance came. Finally, on 10 March 1876, reflecting upon the expectations of Ichizaemon, Yutaka boarded the 1200-ton commercial liner, Oceanic, at Yokohama Port—bound for the United States. It has been 18 years since Ichizaemon, deeply concerned with the monetary outflow, decided to take up foreign trade.

Shortly before Yutaka's departure, inspired by their ambitions, the brothers founded "Morimura Gumi", a pioneer in Japan's foreign trade industry. At that time Ichizaemon was 38-years-old and Yutaka was 23-years-old. It was spring and the cherry trees were in blossom.

After furthering his study of commerce in the United States for 6 months, Yutaka opened a retail store on Front Street, New York in September 1876, marking the first step in the long-cherished trade between Japan and the United States. In 1877 he expanded his business by starting a new company, Hinode Shokai, at 238 6th Street, New York with the help of a partner. After terminating this partnership in 1878, Yutaka independently founded "Morimura Bros." Thus, Morimura Gumi was established in New York, in name and in fact.

Pure White Challenge

Since then, Morimura Gumi has been continuously active in foreign trade for almost a century. Meanwhile, an epochmaking event occurred which is worth of special note.

In 1883 Yutaka shipped a French-made coffee cup to Japan from the United States with a note saying that it was of utmost importance to begin domestic production of such cups. He considered these cups to be highly suitable for the US market and envisioned that they would be of great help in developing future markets in the United States.

At that time, the ceramics industry in Japan had no experience with this type of coffee cup. Even some of the leading potteries did not possess the necessary production technology. Since there were imperative requirements for Morimura Gumi to achieve this plan, extensive studies were carried out in collaboration with a potter in Seto, and birth was given to the first successful production of porcelain coffee cups in Japan. Mormura Gumi then committed all its resources to the task of producing hard, white porcelain ware, with the objective of modernizing the chinaware industry.

On 1 January 1904, just before the Russo-Japanese War, the chief executives of Morimura Gumi, encouraged by their success in producing white porcelain ware after a series of research trips to European countries, founded "Nippon Toki Gomei Kaisha", bearing the future expectations of the company. This was a forerunner of the present "Noritake Co., Limited".

The principal office of Nippon Toki Gomei Kaisha was then located in a village called Noritake (now Noritake Shin-machi, Nishi-ku, Nagoya City). Tradition says that this site was once a rice field belonging to a powerful, feudal clan called the Noritakes. Noritake China, which later became world famous, derives its name from the village where the company was located.

In May 1916 Toyo Toki K.K. (presently TOTO Limited) was established as a subsidiary, to pioneer in domestic production of ceramic sanitary ware. Three years later in May 1919, "Nippon Gaishi K.K." (presently NGK Insulators, Limited) was founded for domestic production of high-tension insulators. In 1936 "Nippon Tokushu Togyo K.K." (presently NGK Spark Plug Co., Limited) was established, equipped with a wide range of production capabilities for ignition plugs, filters, and acid proof mortar.

Thus, a series of subsidiaries have been instrumental in the prosperity of the so-called "Morimura Group". The ideal of national prosperity on the basis of foreign trade, which Ichizaemon cherished in his heart, continued to guide these companies and has been handed down from generation to generation. In April 1917 Morimura Gumi was reorganized as "Morimura Gumi K.K." as a so called holding company for the purpose of managing investments. In October 1919 Morimura Bros. was consolidated into Morimura Gumi K.K. which, as the holding company, controlled its subsidiaries till the end of World War II.

Thus, Morimura Gumi experienced its first prewar golden-age period. Regretfully, however, Ichizaemon Morimura VI passed away on 11 September 1919 at the age of 81. His second son, Kaisaku Morimura, succeeding him as family head and was renamed Ichizaemon Morimura VII in 1928.

In recognition of his achievements as a businessman, Ichizaemon Morimura VI, founder of our present-day company, was conferred the title of Baron. Late in life, he founded "Morimura School" and "Japan Women's University", contributing to the education of the future generations. He also devoted himself to the Salvation Army, serving faithfully as an evangelist. His spiritualism has been imparted in and out of his business. His beliefs, set down on his 81st, years old which have been handed down and adopted are quoted below.

Creed of Our Company

I. This company was established in order to recognize the brotherhood of human beings, to keep the peace of the world, to bring happiness to everyone and to practice justice and humanity by means of the foreign trade business.

II. You should not look after your own interests but aim at prosperity for coming generations at the sacrifice of yourselves.

III. You should aim at absolute sincerity and faithfulness and not break any promise.

IV. You should refrain from lies, self-conceit, anger, haughtiness and idleness.

V. You must uphold integrity in every way and at any cost. A friend is a more valuable treasure than a blood relation and through the co-operation of our friends we can achieve much more work than might be achieved by the use of money. Friendships must be kept forever.

VI. You should feel positive that, believing in God, everything is possible.

You should keep the above resolutions with an iron will and try to be a light of the world.

Ichizaemon Morimura

New Start—Japan Defeated

On 15 August 1945, World War II (often referred to as the biggest tragedy for humanity in this century) finally came to an end. It had been a long, hard war for Japan, lasting 14 long years from the outbreak of the Manchurian Incident.

Although eagerly-awaited peace returned, Japan's economy was in a state of total ruin, aggravated by an incredibly high inflation rate. Under such circumstances, business enterprises were obliged to scramble for business in order to survive.

The immediate postware period was extremely severe for Morimura Gumi. In fact, it was a question of survival for the Company. All assets of Morimura Bros. in New York were frozen. Noritake Co., Limited and the other subsidiary companies were obliged to steer independent courses, affected by dissolution of the big financial combines (Zaibatsu) and enforcement of the deconcentration act under the occupation policy. Morimura Gumi was forced to release the majority of its shareholdings and break off relations with its subsidiaries one by one.

Thus the pages of our painful postwar history were turned. In July 1946 "Morimura Gumi K.K." was renamed "Morimura Shoji K.K." in accord with modern times and to make a fresh start with a new mental outlook.

The time was ripe for developing and promoting new business. In the autumn of 1950 a Special Products Division consisting of only three members, including President

Takao Morimura who was then a newcomer, was formed to find a way out of prevailing difficulties by shifting from exportation to importation.

The first success in marketing imported goods was with a ceramic opacifier called "ULTROX". Thereafter, intensive and desperate efforts were made to open new marketing fields for imported goods. By 1955 the Company had succeeded in laying a foundation for import trade.

In April 1960 "Morimura-Chemetron, Limited" was established between "Chemetron Corporation, USA" and the Company as equal partners, followed by "M & T Japan, Limited" which was established under joint management by "M & T Chemical Inc., USA", the "Nippon Chemical Industrial Co., Limited", and the Company. In August 1972 "The Harshaw Chemical Co., USA", "Murata Chemical Co., Limited", and the Company established a joint venture company called "Harshaw Murata Co., Limited." In December of the same year, establishment of "Moralco Limited" was realized between the Company and "Aluminum Company of America," the largest aluminum maker in the world.

In December 1960 "Morimura Real Estate Co., Limited", a wholly owned subsidiary of Morimura Bros., Inc. completed construction of the 9-story "Morimura Building" at Shiba Kotohiracho, Minato-ku, Tokyo. A new era was begun, with this building as the company's principal office. Since that time, the Company has pursued an active policy for improving and expanding its domestic sales network, while at the same time, setting up affiliates on a joint venture basis with leading firms abroad, so that successful entry could be made into the manufacturing field.

The Spirit of the Founder Lives On

Today, the Company's joint venture activities are doing well, and all 10 of the former subsidiary companies, the so-called Morimura Group, such as Noritake Co., Limited, TOTO Limited, NGK Insulators, Limited, NGK Spark Plug Co., Limited and so on are enjoying increasing prosperity.

There is a strong kindred spirit amongst the Group, and the individual companies cooperate with each other in expanding their businesses. The presidents of each company act as Board Members in the other companies, and in the spring and autumn of each year, the directors of the Group get together to renew their friendships and to exchange ideas and information.

In a word, the entire Group is enjoying prosperity in each activity, stemming from observance of the spirit of Baron Morimura.

In closing, we are proud of our past history and solemnly declare that we will continue to strive hard for national prosperity through foreign trade in the spirit of our forebears, that is, the "Creed of Our Company."

The Noritake Company

The history of the Noritake Co., Limited (Nippon Toki Kabushiki Kaisha), Noritake, Nagoya, Japan was compiled in February, 1968 mainly for the important clients to the Noritake factory from foreign countries. The Noritake Co. has graciously consented to share this information and the following has been adapted from it.

The Noritake Company was founded in 1904 and has devoted itself to making fine china and beauty for gourmet tables around the world. Noritake has not been content however to rest on its international reputation and is constantly refining its technologies and innovating new chinaware.

Their model plant is located in Nagoya, Japan and each stage of Noritake porcelain can be seen from the mixing of the clay to moulding, glazing, firing and painting. Samples of Noritake china which have been exported can also be viewed in the museum.

The founder of Noritake was Baron Ichizaemon Morimura who was born in 1839 in a family of merchants who acted as purveyors to feudal lords. In 1860 when he was twenty years old the shogunate decided that a delegation be sent to the United States to return the courtesy visit of Commodore Perry.

Baron Morimura was ordered to change Japanese money into American coin in the Yokohama foreign concession for the delegation to carry to the United States.

The Japanese money to be exchanged was gold coin of high purity, while the currency to be received was coin of very low quality called Mexican silver.

The late Baron I. Morimura felt that it was great loss to the country to allow gold of such high purity to flow out of Japan and spoke about the matter to Yukichi Fukuzawa, one of the great leaders in the modernization of New Japan from the feudal shogunate-governing era.

Fukuzawa told Morimura that it was necessary to promote the export trade so that the gold coin that went out of Japan would flow back into the country.

Ichizaemon Morimura founded Morimura Bros., Inc. at Ginza in Tokyo in 1876 and started a trading firm in exporting traditional Japanese style of pottery, bamboo works and other Japanese gift items and so-called Japanese sundry goods to the United States. He aimed at having export trade and branched out into another retail and wholesale office in New York City in 1877.

During its expansion of export business, Morimura Bros. decided to concentrate on ceramics, thus Noritake was founded by him on January 1, 1904 at the present site of the main factory for the primary purpose of manufacturing and exporting high quality chinaware mainly to the United States. Since then the United States has been the biggest customer for Noritake.

The founders were Ichizaemon Morimura, Magobei Okura, Jitsuei Hirose, Yasukata Murai, Kazuchika Okura and Kotaro Asukai.

The technique to manufacture high quality dinnerware was mastered in the 1910's and Noritake adopted a streamlined mass production system in the twenties and thirties and enjoyed the high reputation of Noritake china all over the world.

During World War II, the main chinaware factory in Nagoya was seriously damaged and the employees were reduced from 4,000 to 1,000. However, right after the War, the United States 8th Army and the Allied Occupation Forces who knew the fine quality of Noritake China came into Japan and set up a Procurement Office to supply the needs for their Troop Housing Program as well as the Dependent House Program.

To comply with this demand which was big enough to rehabilitate the factory, Noritake had resumed manufacturing chinaware with the assistance of GHQ Industrial Division, Aichi Prefectural Military Government, QMC of Tokai Region and so forth who helped Noritake obtain the raw materials, fuels, liquid gold, packing materials, etc. and also issued to Noritake huge blanket orders for financing and recovering purpose.

This helped the Noritake Company recover rapidly and increased the production and improved its quality.

In 1946 and 1947, Noritake did not like to supply the U.S. Military personnel with items under the brand name of "Noritake", but named it "Rose China" since Noritake did not have the confidence that it could produce the high quality of pre-war standard items that deserved to be named Noritake. There was a shortage of superior raw materials, equipment and skillful employees at this time and Noritake did not want to spoil its high reputation of the Noritake name that it had established in the pre-war days in the United States. The U.S. Procurement Office understood their situation and accepted their supply of Rose China until 1948.

During the course of resumption of foreign trade with the United States and other countries in and after 1948, Noritake expanded itself extensively to become the largest chinaware manufacturer in the world and completed the new Miyoshi Dinner Ware Plant in 1965 in the eastern end of Aichi Prefecture which was equipped with revolutionary modern mechanical processes.

The Noritake Company has a number of offices in the United States and has grown from its humble beginning in 1904 to a company known all over the world for its fine china.

Trade Names and Addresses in New York, N.Y.

MORIMURA BROS. & CO.
MORIMURA BROS.
MORIMURA BROS., INC.

———————————— o ———————————— o ————————————

1876	#97, Front Street (Retailing) (HINODE SHOKAI, formed in November)		
1877	(HINODE SHOKAI, Fulton Street, (w/ - Mr. M. Sato))		
1878	(HINODE SHOKAI, 238, 6th Avenue, (w/ - Mr. M. Sato))		
1879	#238, 6th Avenue	(M.B. & CO.)	
1881	221, 6th Avenue	(M.B. & CO.)	
1884	541, Broadway	(M. Bros.)	(Wholesaler)
1890	530, Broadway	(M. Bros.)	(Wholesaler)
1894	538, Broadway	(M. Bros.)	(Wholesaler)
1902	546, Broadway	(M. Bros.)	(Wholesaler)
1917	53-57, West 23rd Street	(M. Bros.)	(Wholesaler)
1921	53-57, West 23rd Street	(M.B. INC.)	
1941	Closed	(M.B. INC.)	
1976	Re-Opened	(M.B. INC.)	
	155, East 55th Street, New York City		

———————————————————————————————

NORITAKE CO., INC.

———————————— o ———————————— o ————————————

1947	#125, East 23rd Street	(N. C. I.)
1951	212, 5th Avenue	(N. C. I.)
1974	41, Madison Avenue	(N. C. I.)

HISTORY OF NORITAKE

1858   Japan signed the Friendship and Commerce Treaty, with U.S.A., Netherland, Russia, United Kingdom and France.

1868   The Shogunate, ended and Meiji era began.

1876   Morimura-Kumi, formed in Tokyo for exporting.
(The Morimuras & The Okuras joined.)

         The Hinode Company, established in New York City for retailing.

1879   The Hinode Company, closed.

         Morimura Bros. & Co., established in New York City.

1880   The Hiroses joined Morimura-Kumi, Tokyo.

1882   Morimura Bros. & Co. decided to be the wholesaler.

1884   Morimura-Kumi arranged to have the subcontract decorating shops in Tokyo, Nagoya & Kyoto.

1904   The Nippon Toki Kaisha, Ltd., established at 510, Mukai, Noritake, Takaha-mura, Aichi-gun, Aichi-ken.
(Now, 3-1-36 , Noritake Shinmachi, Nishi-ku, Nagoya, Japan)
(The English name was changed to Noritake Co., Limited in 1963.)

1916   Nitto Shokai, established in Nagoya for the home market.
(Now, Noritake Sales, Ltd.)

1917   The Toyo Toki Kaisha, Ltd., established at Kokura to produce Earthen-ware, Chinaware & Sanitary-ware.
(Now, Toto Ltd.)

1918   Morimura-Kumi, reorganized as Morimura Bros., Inc.

1919   The Nippon Gaishi Kaisha, Ltd., established in Nagoya.
(Now, NGK Insulators, Ltd.)

         Okura Art China, established in Tokyo.
(Now, Okura China, Inc.)

1921   Morimura Bros., New York, merged in Morimura Bros., Inc. Tokyo.
Ina Seito Kaisha, Ltd., established in Tokoname.
(Now, Ina Seito Company Limited)

1926   Nitto Yoko, established in Semarang.

Noritake (CURRENT) (BACK STAMPS)	*Noritake* since 1904 JAPAN	明治三十七年創業
Noritake x 75th 1979 ANNIVERSARY JAPAN	*Noritake* N ® JAPAN	NO.175 HAND PAINTED NORITAKE ® MADE IN JAPAN
Noritake Ivory China N ® JAPAN	*Noritake* BONE CHINA ® JAPAN	*Noritake* Studio Collection N JAPAN BONE CHINA

15

1930	Nitto Yoko, established in Soerabaja.
1936	The Kyoritsu Yogyo Kaisha, Ltd., established in Nagoya. (Now, Kyoritsu Ceramic Materials Co., Ltd.)
	The Nitto Sekko Kaisha, Ltd., established in Nagoya. (Now, Nitto Gypsum Co., Ltd.)
	Nippon Tokushu Togyo Kabushiki Kaisha, established in Nagoya. (Now, NGK Spark Plug Co., Ltd.)
1939	Started to produce Grinding Wheels.
1947	Noritake Co., Inc., established in New York City.
1956	Started to produce Stainless Steel Flatware.
1958	Noritake (Australia) Pty. Limited, established in Sydney.
	Noritake Co., Limited and Toto Ltd. contracted the production agreement with Gladdin McBean & Co., U.S.A. (Brand name : Franciscan)
1961	Started to produce Crystal Glassware.
	Started to produce Melamine Ware.
1962	Started to produce Grinding & Ceramic Machines.
1963	Started to produce Coated Abrasives.
1969	Started to produce Electronic Parts.
1971	Started to produce Earthenware.
	Started to produce Stoneware.
1972	Started to produce Clay Pipe.
	Noritake Togei, established in Kyushu. Lanka Porcelain Limited, established in Sri Lanka.
1973	Started to produce Diamond Tools.
1974	Porcelana Mariwasa Inc, established in Philippines.
1975	Noritake Ireland Limited, established in Ireland.
1979	Noritake Model Plant opened.
1981	The Company's Japanese name changed to Noritake Co,Limited.

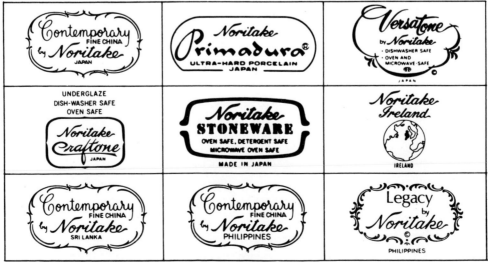

Noritake Co. Presidents

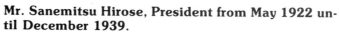

Mr. Kazuchika Okura, President of Noritake from 1904 until May 1922.

Mr. Sanemitsu Hirose, President from May 1922 until December 1939.

Mr. Ippei Iino, Noritake's President from December 1939 until November 1942.

A Trip To The Noritake Museum In Nagoya

All of these pieces were produced in the 1910's during the Nippon era and are on display in the Noritake Museum. (Courtesy Noritake Company)

This photo is of the first dinner plate manufactured in the Noritake factory in 1914. It is pattern D1441 "Sedan". The backstamp is Noritake, M in wreath, hand painted, Nippon. (Courtesy Noritake Company)

Matching pieces in Sedan pattern. (Photo supplied by a collector.)

This particular pattern was designed by Frank Lloyd Wright, the famous American architect. He also designed the hotel it was to be used in, the Imperial Hotel in Tokyo, Japan. He was one of the greatest architects of modern times. He began to design buildings with simple, bold lines and designed the Imperial Hotel so that it would withstand earthquakes. According to records the hotel was literally a tourist attraction during the construction period and caused quite a sensation. It was finished in 1922 and although it rested on a bed of soft mud it suffered no damage in the big 1923 earthquake.

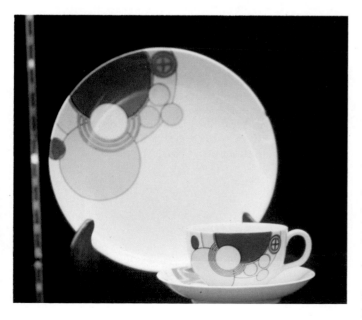

According to the Noritake Co. the date of production was always marked underneath the backstamp and this particular china was manufactured for the hotel over and over again. They tell me that although there is no record left with them to confirm the date of the first production, it is natural to guess it was around 1922, judging from the facts that the remodeling designed by Mr. Wright was completed in 1922 and about the same time the china design was also done by him.

I contacted The Frank Lloyd Wright Memorial Foundation in Scottsdale, Arizona for further information regarding this china. They say that this design is for the china used in the Grille and Cabaret. Another, more "conservative" design was used in the Main Dining Room. All chinaware for the hotel was not manufactured following the date of the demolition of the building in 1967-68. The Foundation has many pieces which date from 1935, 1952, 1962 and 1966, the various times that they ordered it from the Noritake Company.

Besides the year of manufacture these pieces (shown in photo) are backstamped RC, "Yajirobe", Noritake, Nippon Toki Kaisha. (Courtesy Noritake Company)

All of the pieces in this photo are of luster wares. The first teapot was manufactured in the 1910's with a backstamp of R.C. underneath a laurel. The rest of the pieces were manufactured in 1928 and are backstamped Noritake, M in wreath, hand painted, made in Japan. (Courtesy of Noritake Company)

This item was manufactured during 1936 through 1945 and bears the Noritake China M with crown mark. The Noritake Co. does not know when this mark started or ended but that it also appears on other dinner sets all of which have been collected from Australia. Backstamp #56. (Courtesy Noritake Company)

This is pattern D6500, "Glenwood", manufactured in 1939. The backstamp is Noritake, M, Japan. (Courtesy Noritake Company)

This piece was manufactured in 1938 with the Noritake China with crown mark. Backstamp #56. (Courtesy Noritake Company)

The comport was manufactured in 1931 and the backstamp is written in Japanese characters meaning "specially made by Nippon Toki Kaisha". The covered box is one of the same time period. (Courtesy Noritake Company)

This bone china pattern is listed as D129 and was manufactured around 1940. The backstamp is Royale Bone China, hand painted, Japan. (Courtesy Noritake Company)

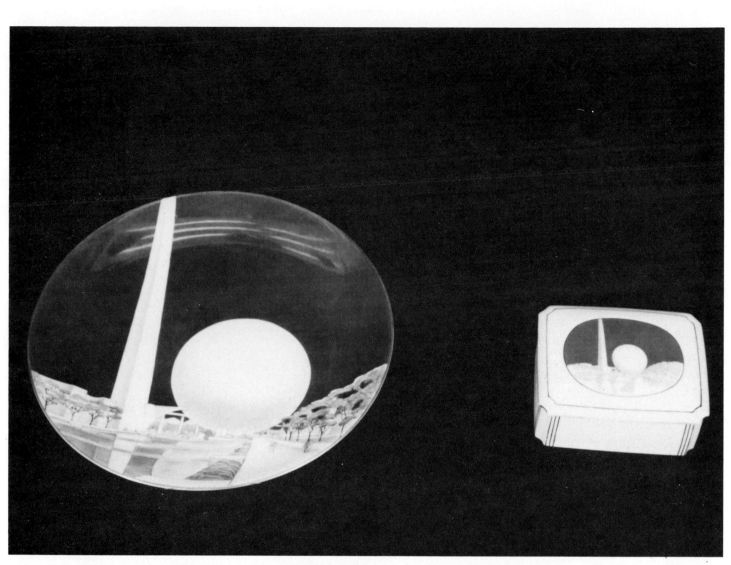

Both of these items were specially made in commemoration of the New York World Fair in 1939. The backstamp of the plate is Noritake mark #38 and the covered box is #78. (Courtesy Noritake Company)

Both the dresser set and vase bear backstamp #7. (Courtesy Noritake Company)

This photo hangs on the wall of the museum and is a 1879 photograph of the New York City store of the Morimura Bros.

A view inside the museum. The walls have built-in display cases for items and there are also four cases in the center of the room.

In the museum cabinet is an old salesman's sample book. It is quite large in size but was evidently folded and put in the salesman's case or back pocket when traveling. He could show the buyer exactly what he would be getting when he bought pieces of Noritake. Each page contains a hand painted work of art of one or more pieces of the wares offered for sale. Rather than traveling around with boxes of coffee pots, humidors, tea sets, etc. he could show the prospective buyer the exact shape and pattern of the pieces. The realism shown in these paintings is awesome. Each is a faithful copy of the original piece. The books contained not only the dinnerware items but also so-called giftware. These books were found by chance in the Noritake Company's stack room but they do not know which designs were actually adopted and which were not. They have no further information about them.

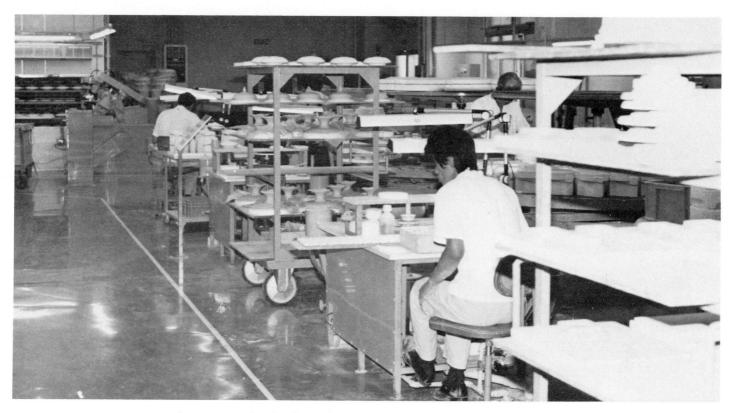

A view inside the first floor of the "model plant" in Nagoya.

This photo was taken on the third floor of the "model plant" and shows pieces in various stages of hand decorating.

Items displayed in museum cases.

One of the vases offered for sale in the shop where the tour of the "modern factory" begins.

A formal dinner table has been set and is in the middle of the museum.

This presentation piece was made especially for the "ribbon cutting" ceremony which opened the museum in 1979 (the American Ambassador to Japan cut the ribbon). This particular piece took three months to produce and most of that time was spent with the decorating.

Okura Art China

(Information courtesy of the Noritake Co., Ltd)

The Okura Art China (now Okura China, Inc.) was founded in 1919 in the suburbs of Tokyo for the purpose of creating and manufacturing such a genuine art china as to be ranked with the leading European art china makers of those days.

The founders were Magobei Okura and his son Kazuchika Okura who also were the founders of Nippon Toki Kaisha (now Noritake Co., Limited). The first product came out of the kiln in 1922. Since then the products have become more popular each year, especially among the upper society including the Imperial House and his family and government offices. Its quality was based on the white body formed by selected quality materials and fired at an exceptionally high temperature and the characteristic designs to which various techniques were applied. The wares still have the same reputation and are still commissioned for the Imperial House.

Their activities in export markets, on the other hand, were not to be compared with the ones in the domestic market. One reason was that their factory was not of the mass production type like Noritake's but of a smaller type called a craftsmen shop and therefore the production capacity was very limited. It must have been the same for their exporting to the United States as the following are the only events I have been able to locate regarding them.

1927: The wares were exhibited at the Philadelphia International Fair and won the Best Prize. It is supposed that this was the first time that their products were introduced into the United States.

1933: Various tablewares were exported for the first time on a commercial basis. Details as to what and whom were not recorded.

1937: Sample pieces were shipped to Morimura Bros. in N.Y.C. for the first time to meet their trial order.

Home sets (composed items unknown) for Carson Piric Scott & Co. in Chicago and bird plaques for Waikiki Bird Park were also shipped in this year.

1940: Various tablewares were shipped to Mitsukoshi House in Honolulu.

Some of the following backstamps contain the year of production but the company has no records as to when this system ended and how it was handled in the early years.

These dinner ware pieces are representative of the Okura China, Inc. product. (Courtesy of Okura China, Inc.)

Backstamps of Okura Art China

款

   (FOR DOMESTIC USE ONLY)

FOUNDED

 CURRENT

JAPAN

The Larkin Connection

The Larkin Co. of Buffalo, N.Y. played a big part in distributing Noritake wares in the United States. Discovered in a fiftieth anniversary catalog printed in 1925 was the following:

"On May 1, 1875, a young man, John D. Larkin, founded in Buffalo, a small two-story factory, 25 by 60 ft., that was destined to cover over 75 acres of floor space.

Tiny was the initial plant that housed the Factory-to-Family idea, and equally small was the first list of Larkin Products when compared with the hundreds comprising the list today.

Toilet and laundry soaps were in the beginning the sole products. Next came soap powders, perfumes, pure foods, etc. and all the widely varied lines that today are represented in the 900 Larkin products whose quality wins for them a welcome among a million American home-makers."

The famous Azalea pattern was given out as premium by the Larkin Co. for many years. Collectors can also credit them for the Sheridan, Tree in the Meadow, Savoy, Briarcliff, Modjeska, Linden, Raised gold and others. A number of them were an exclusive with the company.

Knowing what an important part the Larkin Co. played in Noritake's destiny, I wrote to the Buffalo and Erie County Public Library, the home town of the Larkins, for further information about the family and company. Barbara M. Soper, librarian, History Department sent me an essay she had printed a few years ago to serve as a quick information source on the famous old soap company. The essay was written under the auspices of the library and was designed to serve the informational needs of library users and correspondents. I wish to thank both the library and Barbara Soper for allowing me to reprint it and share it with readers of this book.

The Larkin Company

Buffalo, New York

The Larkin Company, founded in 1875, was once a giant of Buffalo area industry. It had a huge manufacturing complex of factories and warehouses in Buffalo as well as branches in cities like Philadelphia, Chicago, Peoria, Cleveland, Boston, and New York.

The Larkin Company started out as a soap manufacturing company, producing laundry soap and toilet soap to be sold through mail-order catalogs. To promote the sale of packages of soap, the company began offering premiums such as a handkerchief in packages of toilet soap and a bath towel in boxes of laundry soap. For the late 1800's, this was a unique idea which, over a period of years, brought great fame and fortune to the company and gave it the financial base to expand into countless other areas.

The firm was headed by Buffalo born John D. Larkin (1845-1926) who, after working for a soap manufacturing company in Chicago for a number of years, had decided to return to Buffalo and establish a business of his own. His first factory was a small building at 199 Chicago Street which produced bars of soap to be sold by pushcarts along the streets of Buffalo. By 1876, the business had expanded to a three-story plant on Seneca Street. It was incorporated as J.D. Larkin and Company with Larkin as President and his brother-in-law, Elbert Hubbard (1856-1915), as Secretary and Treasurer.

The Hubbard genius for descriptive writing and sales promotion became the firm's greatest asset. Celebrated in literary, philosophical, and avant-garde circles of the time, Hubbard was also an astute businessman who applied his literary talents unabashedly to the field of advertising. It was Hubbard who pioneered the idea of a three cake box of soap which had broader appeal to the public than the 12 cake box which was previously offered. He also devised an early form of installment buying by selling "Combination Boxes" to the public at a price of $6.00. The box contained 100 cakes of Sweet Home Soap, and the purchaser, in addition to receiving a premium, was allowed 30 days in which to pay the $6.00. Hubbard originated the name "Cream Oatmeal Soap" which was one of the company's biggest sellers. He also introduced a wide range of additional premiums such as silver-plated teaspoons, napkin rings, and butter plates.

By the turn of the century the Larkin Company was a phenomenal success, not only because of Hubbard's advertising genius, but because of John Larkin's sales philosophy. Larkin's basic approach to marketing was to cut out middlemen and brokers and to sell directly to the consumer. He called this the "factory to family" sales method. His aim was to cut all cost that added no value to the product being marketed and to pass the savings along to the buyer in the form of premiums. A $10.00 purchase of soap would entitle the customer to a $10.00 premium. If an individual purchased enough Larkin products over the years, he could conveniently furnish a home with the ever expanding array of Larkin premiums. The business acumen of Larkin and Hubbard was largely responsible for the fact that Buffalo in 1900 was the second largest soap manufacturing city in the world.

The Larkin sales philosophy became so popular with the public that housewives devised their own group sales plans to promote the Larkin products. These "Larkin Clubs" were usually groups of 10 housewives who collectively agreed to purchase a bulk shipment of Larkin products valued at $10.00. Since none of the ladies could use the entire shipment of soap or afford the total price, they each agreed to buy $1.00 worth per month and then draw lots for the $10.00 premium. At the end of 10 months, each woman would have received $10.00 worth of soap products and also a premium. "Larkin Clubs" proliferated over the American landscape, boosting Larkin sales to unprecedented heights. Over a 25 year period, the company managed to sell one and a half million bars of toilet soap and 175 million boxes of laundry soap.

After 1900, the Larkin Company began to respond to mail-order customers' demands for a wide range of products other than soap. The firm began the manufacture of perfumes and pharmaceuticals. A line of packaged foods such as coffee, tea, extracts, and bakery products was introduced around 1905. This was followed by a line of paints and varnishes which eventually led to the manufacture of furniture.

Furniture production at the Larkin Company began around 1911. A furniture company in Memphis, Tennessee initially produced furniture parts and sent them to Buffalo for finishing. The arrangement with the Memphis firm was dissolved at a later date, however, and all operations connected with furniture manufacture took place in Buffalo. Many of the furniture pieces such as the famous Chautauqua desks, chairs, lamps, and stoves were offered as premiums to promote the company's soap products.

Furniture items as premiums had great appeal in small towns and rural areas which was the heartland of Larkin sales territory. People in such areas lacked the ready cash to purchase household furnishings, and were very appreciative of the furniture items offered as premiums. Sales from the company's mail-order catalogs continued to skyrocket even as local furniture manufacturers protested the invasion of their markets. These angry merchants pointed out that it would be more appropriate to offer soap products as a premium for furniture purchases, rather than the other way around.

The Larkin Company, nevertheless, committed itself to a policy of offering increasingly valuable items as premiums. By 1909, two large catalogs were published each year to picture and describe the 900 premiums available to the public. These catalogs received national circulation, and the orders that they produced were so overwhelming that the U.S. Post Office had to set up a branch within the Larkin building. The Larkin premium catalog became known as the "Book of a Million Homes."

Since many pottery and china items became very popular as premiums, John D. Larkin was encouraged to establish a pottery in Buffalo to produce them in large quantities. In 1903, the first kiln was fired in a building at Seneca and Hayes Place which became known as the Buffalo Pottery. The pottery developed into a giant manufacturing complex of its own, turning out exquisite plates, pitchers, jugs, bowls, and wall plaques. Some of the famous dinnerware patterns produced at the pottery from 1904 to 1921 included "Bonrea," "Princess," "Tea Rose," "Seneca," "Minerva," "Rosebank," "Dresden," and "Glendale." The pottery also produced a vast array of specialty items such as Christmas plates, historical plates, dresser trays, tea trays, and punch bowls.

During the First World War, the Larkin pottery supplied the U.S. Army and Navy with china for use in military hospitals and aboard merchant ships. At the War's end, the pottery went back to producing dinnerware for use as premiums, or for sale directly to the public. Its highest art line was Deldare Ware which was produced at the pottery from 1908 to 1925. Deldare Ware was offered only once as a premium in the fall-winter catalog of 1922-1923. In the late 1920's, as production costs mounted and prices rose, the average man found the products produced by the Buffalo Pottery to be beyond his financial reach. The pottery, therefore, turned to the manufacture of china for hotel and institutional use, and the Larkin Company relied on cheaper imported china to meet its premium needs.

The Larkin name continued to be associated with catalogs and the mail-order business, but around 1918, the firm established a string of retail stores. At this point, company executives realized that the firm was manufacturing more commodities than the mail-order business could consume. It had branched into the textile industry and was marketing women's housedresses and children's apparel as well as a line of men's clothing manufactured by the closely affiliated Buffalo Garment Company. It was also retailing a variety of leather products produced by the Buffalo Leather Goods Company, and a giant assortment of baked goods turned out by the Larkin Company's own bakery.

A string of 103 chain stores eventually grew up in the Buffalo area to merchandise the Larkin commodities. These stores served territory within a 150 mile radius of Buffalo, and each was headed by a general manager. Most of the sales in these retail outlets consisted of foodstuffs which, by 1918, accounted for one third of the firm's total volume of business. A Larkin Market was opened in 1929 to further dispense these foodstuffs. The market offered a telephone shopping service whereby girls at the market took grocery orders from the public and then filled the orders from the market's inventories.

The Larkin Administration Building, a gigantic, futuristic building designed by architect Frank Lloyd Wright was one of the most celebrated buildings of its time. It was one of the largest private office buildings in the world, and was hailed as an architectural marvel both in the United States and in Europe. One of the twelve largest pipe organs in the world was housed within the building, and it provided daily music for the firm's 1,800 clerks, typists, and executives.

The Larkin manufacturing complex in Buffalo became a tourist attraction for travellers from all over America as well as for foreign visitors. In 1908, more than 50,000 people took the conducted tour through the Larkin buildings. These visitors had the opportunity to see the nerve center of the Larkin operation from an area in the Administration Building known as "inspiration point." The King and Queen of Belgium once honored Buffalo and the Larkin executives by a royal visit to the company's headquarters. They were, undoubtedly, as awestruck as the other guests to see the fantastic manufacturing empire that had started from a bar of soap.

The Larkin Company has now been out of business for 35 years. Its fortunes steadily declined in the late 1920's and early 1930's as it faced stiff competition from the expanding chain store movement in the United States, and also from rival mail-order firms. The sales methods that appealed to rural Americans living in isolated communities at the turn of the century had lesser appeal to the urban Americans of a later age who preferred to shop in person at a department store than to order merchandise from a mail-order catalog. The Larkin Administration Building, symbol of a bygone age and a vanished industrial empire, fell to the wrecking ball in 1950.

Barbara Soper
History Department
Buffalo & Erie County Public Library
October, 1976

Sources:

The *Book of Buffalo Pottery*, Altman, Violet & Seymour
(New York: Crown) ©1969

The Larkin Company: a history, Schlei, Mildred B.
(Master's Thesis University of Buffalo) 1932

As well as collecting porcelain items I have also managed to purchase a number of old trade catalogs. These catalogs prove to be a wealth of information to collectors as they fill us in on the history of these pieces. I have been lucky enough to purchase many of the old Larkin catalogs and these cover the years of 1917-1918, also 1923-1940. The following information was gathered from these specific catalogs.

The azalea pattern is described as hand painted thin white china decorated with hand painted pink and white azaleas and green leaves, edges outlined in gold and handles gold traced. Pieces were added and dropped during the years so I have chosen several old ads when necessary to show all the items sold.

Azalea #2, cup and saucer, dates advertised 1917-40.

Azalea #3, whipped cream set, 4½″ bowl, ladle and plate, dates advertised 1917-33.

Azalea #4, 7½″ tea plate, dates advertised 1917-40.

Azalea #7, sugar bowl, 3-5/8″ tall and cream, 3-1/8″ tall, advertised between the years of 1923-33.

Azalea #8, bread and butter plate, 6½″ in diameter, advertised from 1925-40.

Azalea #9, fruit saucer, 5¼″ in diameter, dates advertised 1925-40.

Azalea #10, 9¾″ cake plate, dates advertised 1925-40.

Azalea #11, salt and pepper shaker set, 3½″ tall, advertised between the years of 1925-27.

Azalea #12, 12″ salad bowl, dates advertised 1925-40.

Azalea #13, 9¾″ wide dinner plate, advertised between 1925-40.

Azalea #14, condiment set, dates advertised 1925-33.

Azalea #15, teapot, 4½″ tall, advertised between 1925-33.

Azalea #17, platter, 10¼″ x 14″, dates advertised 1925-40.

Azalea #18, relish dish, 8¼″ long, dates advertised 1925-29.

Azalea #19, soup plate, 7-1/8″ in diameter, dates advertised 1925-40.

Azalea #39, refreshment set, dates advertised 1926-32.

Azalea #40, gravy boat, 8½″ long, dates advertised 1926-40.

Azalea #54, butter tub, 5-1/8″ diameter, dates advertised 1927-36.

Azalea #55, oatmeal dish, 5¾″ diameter, dates advertised 1927-40.

Azalea #56, platter, 9″ x 12″, dates advertised 1927-40.

Azalea #89, salt and pepper shaker set, 3″ tall, dates advertised 1927-40.

Azalea #97, syrup pitcher, 4½″ tall, plate, 5½″ diameter, dates advertised 1928-34.

Azalea #98, 8½″ breakfast plate, dates advertised 1928-40.

Azalea #99, celery or roll tray, advertised between 1928-40.

Azalea #100, one quart jug, 5-5/8″ tall, dates advertised 1928-34.

Azalea #101, open vegetable dish, 10½″ long, dates advertised 1928-33.

Azalea #119, 10″ relish dish, dates advertised 1928-33.

Azalea #120, egg cup, 3-1/8″ tall, dates advertised 1928-34.

Azalea #121, pickle or lemon set, 5½″ diameter, dates advertised 1928-32.

Azalea #122, berry sugar and cream set, sugar is 6½″ tall and cream is 5¾″ tall, dates advertised 1928-34.

Azalea #123, sugar (2½″ tall) and cream (3½″ tall), dates advertised 1928-35.

Azalea #124, bouillon cup (3½″ tall) and saucer (5½″ diameter), dates advertised 1928-40.

Azalea #125, jam jar (5″ tall) and plate (5¼″ diameter), dates advertised 1928-36.

Azalea #126, individual salt and pepper shakers, 2-9/16″ tall, dates advertised 1928-37.

Azalea #169, teapot tile, 6″ wide, dates advertised 1929-40.

Azalea #170, comport, 6½″ in diameter, 2¾″ tall, dates advertised 1929-37.

Azalea #171, two compartment relish dish, 8¼″ long, dates advertised 1929-36.

Azalea #172, vegetable dish, 9¼″ long, dates advertised 1929-40.

Azalea #182, after dinner coffee pot and six cups, dates advertised 1930-33.

Azalea #183, after dinner cup and saucer set, cup 2-1/8″ tall, saucer 4¼″ diameter, dates advertised 1930-31 and 1933.

Azalea #184, bon bon dish, 6¼″ diameter, dates advertised 1930-34.

Azalea #185, grapefruit or candy bowl, 4½″ diameter, dates advertised 1930-33.

Azalea #186, platter 12″ x 16″, dates advertised 1930-40.

Azalea #187, footed vase, 5½″ tall, dates advertised 1930-34.

Azalea #188, nut or fruit bowl, shell shape, 7¾″ long, dates advertised 1930-32.

Azalea #189, spoon holder, 8″ long, dates advertised 1930-35.

Azalea #190, vinegar bottle, 6¼″ tall, dates advertised 1930-34.

Azalea #191, handled mustard with spoon, 1-7/8″ tall,, dates advertised 1930-34.

Azalea #192, match or toothpick holder, 2½″ tall, dates advertised 1930-34.

Azalea #193, Dolly Varden basket, 4-3/8″ long, dates advertised 1930-33.

Azalea #194, relish dish, 8¼″ long, dates advertised 1929-32; relish dish, 7-1/8″ long, dates advertised 1936-40.

Azalea #310, deep bowl, 5-1/8″ diameter, dates advertised 1930-40.

Azalea #311, platter, 10¼″ x 7¼″, dates advertised 1930-40.

Azalea #312, butter chip, 3½″ diameter, dates advertised 1930-33.

Azalea #313, covered candy jar, 5″ tall, dates advertised 1930-34.

Azalea #314, cheese or butter dish, 5″ tall, dates advertised 1930-40.

Azalea #315, fruit or salad plate, 7-5/8″ diameter, dates advertised 1930-40.

Azalea #338, grill plates, 10¼″ diameter, dates advertised 1930-36.

Azalea #363, cream soup set, 5-1/8″ in diameter, dates advertised 1932-40.

Azalea #372, casserole, 10¾″ diameter, dates advertised 1934-40.

Azalea #400, teapot, 4½″ tall, dates advertised 1934-40.

Azalea #401, sugar and cream set, bowl diameter is 3-3/5″, dates advetised 1934-40.

Azalea #439, divided vegetable dish, 9½″ diameter, dates advertised 1935-40.

Azalea #444, celery tray, 10″ long, dates advertised 1937-40.

Azalea #449, sugar and creamer set, 2½″ tall, dates advetised 1937-40.

Azalea #450, twin relish dish, 7½″ long, dates advertised 1937-40.

Azalea #452, vase, 6¼″ tall, dates advertised 1937-40.

Azalea #453, mayonnaise set, bowl is 5½″ diameter, dates advertised 1937-40.

I was unable to obtain a 1941 catalog but it stands to reason that many of these items were also made in that year. Several items were only manufactured for a couple years such as #11, #182, #188, etc. and it will be much more difficult for the collector to find these pieces.

The Tree in the Meadow pattern is another popular one with collectors but is very similar to other patterns. The name "tree in the meadow" was given by collectors as it has no name in the old catalogs. It is a scenic design in rich shades, autumn colors with brown predominating. These pieces were only sold in the Larkin catalogs between the years of 1926-35 and the following is a list of those located.

TIM #41, teapot, 4½″ tall, dates advertised 1926-35.

TIM #42, sugar (3-5/8″ tall) and creamer (3-1/8″ tall), dates advertised 1926-35.

TIM #44, tea plate, 7½″ in diameter, dates advertised 1926-35.

TIM #45, cake plate, 9¾″ in diameter, dates advertised 1926-34.

TIM #46, bread and butter plate, 6½″ in diameter, dates advertised 1926-35.

TIM #47, salad bowl, 10-1/16″ in diameter, dates advertised 1926-34.

TIM #48, fruit saucer, 5¼″ wide, dates advertised 1926-35.

TIM #49, condiment set, tray, salt, pepper, mustard with spoon, dates advertised 1926-35.

TIM #111, breakfast plate, 8½″ in diameter, dates advertised 1928-35.

TIM #113, 12″ long platter, dates advertised 1928-35.

TIM #114, open vegetable, 10½″ long, dates advertised 1928-1935.

TIM #135, pickle set, 5¼″ diameter, dates advertised 1928-35.

TIM #136, jam jar, 5¼″ tall, dates advertised 1928-34.

TIM #137, salt and pepper shakers, 3″ tall, dates advertised 1928-35.

TIM #138, berry sugar (6½″ tall) and cream (5¾″ tall) set, dates advertised 1928-35.

TIM #139, butter tub, 5-1/8″ diameter, dates advertised 1928-33.

TIM #140, refreshment set, dates advertised 1928-33.

TIM #174, teapot tile, 6″ in diameter, dates advertised 1929-31 and 1933.

TIM #175, comport, 6½″ in diameter, dates advertised 1929-35.

TIM #176, compartment relish dish, 8-1/8″ long, dates advertised 1929-35.

TIM #177, open vegetable dish, 9¼″ across handles, dates advertised 1929-33.

TIM #178, after dinner coffee cup and saucer, 2-1/8″ tall, dates advertised 1929-31.

TIM #179, after dinner coffee pot (6 cup capacity), dates advertised 1929-34.

TIM #201, dinner plate, 9¾″ wide, dates advertised 1930-34.

TIM #202, platter, 14″ long, dates advertised 1930-35.

TIM #203, oatmeal dish, 5¾″ wide, dates advertised 1930-35.

TIM #203, sugar (2½″ tall) and cream (3½″ tall) set, dates advertised 1930-33.

TIM #205, relish dish, 5″ x 7″, dates advertised 1930-33.

TIM #206, whipped cream set, 4¼″ bowl, ladle and plate, dates advertised 1930-34.

TIM #207, celery tray, 12″ x 5¾″, dates advertised 1930-35.

TIM #208, individual salt and pepper shakers, 2-9/16″ tall, dates advertised 1930-34.

TIM #209, footed vase, 5½″ tall, dates advertised 1930-35.

TIM #210, nut or fruit bowl, 7¾″ x 6½″, dates advertised 1930-33.

TIM #211, mustard jar, 1-7/8″ tall, dates advertised 1930-31.

TIM #212, match or toothpick holder, 2½″ tall, dates advertised 1930-33.

TIM #213, Dolly Varden basket, 4″ tall, dates advertised 1930-31.

TIM #214, casserole, 10¼" diameter, dates advertised 1930-35.

TIM #215, gravy boat, 8½" long, dates advertised 1930-35.

TIM #216, soup plate, 7-1/8" diameter, dates advertised 1930-34.

TIM #316, deep bowl, 5-1/8" diameter, dates advertised 1930-33.

TIM #317, small platter, 7½" x 10¼", dates advertised 1930-35.

TIM #318, candy jar, 5" tall, dates advertised 1930-34.

TIM #319, vinegar and oil set, 6½" long, dates advertised 1930-35.

TIM #320, cheese or butter dish, diameter of plate is 6½", dates advertised 1930-35.

TIM #321, salad bowl, 8½" across handles, dates advertised 1930-33.

TIM #322, cake plate, 9" diameter, dates advertised 1930-33.

TIM #323, fruit or salad plate, 7-5/8" in diameter, dates advertised 1930-34.

TIM #324, celery and relish dish, 11½" x 6", dates advertised 1932-34.

The "Sheridan" pattern is found advertised in the 1926-35 catalogs. Its decoration is of delicate clusters of flowers and foliage in various colors retouched by hand. The narrow border is light blue and black and the handles and edges are traced in gold.

Sheridan #21, cup and saucer, dates advertised 1926-35.

Sheridan #22, bread and butter plate, 6½" in diameter, dates advertised 1926-35.

Sheridan #23, tea plate, 7½", dates advertised 1926-35.

Sheridan #24, dinner plate, 9¾" in diameter, dates advertised 1926-35.

Sheridan #25, soup plate, 7-3/8" in diameter, dates advertised 1926-35.

Sheridan #26, fruit saucer, 5¼" in diameter, dates advertised 1926-35.

Sheridan #27, platter, 10½" x 14", dates advertised 1926-35.

Sheridan #28, platter, 9" x 12", dates advertised 1926-35.

Sheridan #29, casserole, 10¼" across handles, dates advertised 1926-34.

Sheridan #30, open vegetable dish, 10½" long, dates advertised 1926-35.

Sheridan #32, gravy boat and attached tray, 8½" long, dates advertised 1926-35.

Sheridan #33, pickle dish, 4½" x 8¼", dates advertised 1926-34.

Sheridan #34, cake plate, 9¾" in diameter, dates advertised 1926-34.

Sheridan #35, sugar (3-5/8" tall) and cream (3-1/8" tall) set, dates advertised 1926-35.

Sheridan #36, teapot, 4½" tall, holds five cups, dates advertised 1926-35.

Sheridan #37, oatmeal dish, 5¾" diameter, dates advertised 1926-35.

Sheridan #38, salad bowl, 10" diameter, dates advertised 1926-34.

Sheridan #102, breakfast plate, 8½" in diameter, dates advertised 1928-35.

Sheridan #103, butter tub, 5-1/8" diameter, dates advertised 1928-35.

Sheridan #115, one quart jug, 5¾" tall, dates advertised 1929-35.

Sheridan #116, egg cup, 3-1/8" tall, dates advertised 1929-35.

Sheridan #117, syrup jug, 4½" tall, dates advertised 1929-35.

Sheridan #118, celery tray, 12¼" long, dates advertised 1929-33.

Sheridan #131, relish, 5" x 7", dates advertised 1929-35.

Sheridan #132, after dinner cup and saucer, 2½" tall, dates advertised 1929-35.

Sheridan #133, bouillon cup and saucer set, dates advertised 1928-35.

Sheridan #134, salt and pepper shakers, 3" tall, dates advertised 1928-35.

Sheridan #173, small open vegetable dish, 9¼" across handles, dates advertised 1929-35.

Sheridan #195, pickle set, 5½" diameter, dates advertised 1930-35.

Sheridan #196, berry sugar and cream set, shaker is 6½" tall and cream is 5¾" tall, dates advertised 1930-35.

Sheridan #197, sugar and cream set, sugar is 2½" tall and cream is 3½" tall, dates advertised 1930-35.

Sheridan #198, after dinner coffee pot (six cup size), dates advertised 1930-35.

Sheridan #199, mustard pot, 1-7/8" tall, dates advertised 1930-33.

Sheridan #200, individual salt and pepper shakers, 2-9/16" tall, dates advertised 1930-35.

Sheridan #330, deep bowl, 5-1/8" diameter, dates advertised 1930-35.

Sheridan #331, platter, 7½" x 10¼", dates advertised 1930-34.

Sheridan #332, butter chip, 3¼" diameter, dates advertised 1930-35.

Sheridan #364, cream soup cup, 5-1/8" diameter, can be used on tea plates #23, dates advertised 1932-35.

The "Modjeska" pattern was offered in the 1930-37 Larkin catalogs. It has an ivory border, medallion decoration in delicate blue forget-me-nots, pink roses, green leaves, orange and yellow with black and gold edges and handles.

All pieces were offered for the entire time period of 1930-37.

Modjeska #247, cup and saucer.

Modjeska #248, bread and butter plate, 6½" in diameter.

Modjeska #249, tea plate, 7½" in diameter.

Modjeska #250, dinner plate, 9¾" in diameter.

Modjeska #251, fruit saucer, 5½" in diameter.

Modjeska #252, soup plate, 7½" in diameter.

Modjeska #253, platter, 12" x 9".

Modjeska #254, platter, 10¼" x 14".

Modjeska #255, casserole, 10¼" in diameter.

Modjeska #256, open vegetable dish, 7¾" x 10½".

Modjeska #257, gravy boat, 8½" long.

Modjeska #258, cake plate, 9¾" across handles.

Modjeska #259, salad bowl, 10" in diameter.

Modjeska #260, teapot, holds five cups, 4½" tall.

Modjeska #261, sugar (3-5/8" tall) and cream (3-1/8" tall) set.

Modjeska #262, oatmeal dish, 5½" in diameter.

Modjeska #263, butter tub, 5-1/8" in diameter.

Modjeska #264, celery tray, 5¾" x 12".

Modjeska #265, salt and pepper shaker set, 3" tall.

Modjeska #266, handled relish tray, 7" long.

Modjeska #302, breakfast plate, 8½" in diameter.

Modjeska #303, open vegetable, 9¼" across handles.

Modjeska #304, compartment relish dish, 8¼" long.

Modjeska #305, comport, 6½" diameter.

Modjeska #306, individual salt and pepper shakers, 2-9/16" tall.

Modjeska #338, deep bowl, 5-1/8" diameter.

Modjeska #339, platter, 7½" x 10¼".

"Savoy" and "Briarcliff" dinner sets were offered in the old Larking catalogs but always as sets and not as open stock. Savoy was advertised in the Fall/Winter issue of 1923-24 through the Spring/Summer issue of 1926. The Briarcliff pattern was offered in the Fall/Winter catalog of 1923-24 until the Fall/Winter catalog of 1926-27.

Savoy is described as having a wide ivory border striped with light brown lines. Hand painted medallions of pink roses with green leaves. The pattern is embellished with a narrow blue and black conventional design around the outer edge. Briarcliff was described in the old ad as having a charming border design of dark blue and black interspersed with wreaths of hand painted pink roses and green leaves. A wide band of old ivory edged with black, enhances the beauty of this set. Items included in both sets were bread and butter plates, tea plates, dinner plates, soup plates, fruit saucers, tea cups and saucers, small platter, medium platter, large platter, two-piece casserole, open vegetable dish, gravy boat with fast stand, sugar bowl, cream pitcher, salad bowl and pickle dish.

The "Raised Gold" pattern was found in the 1930-40 catalogs and most likely appeared in the 1941 issue. It has a border of ivory with a touch of orange and blue in the flowers. The raised medallions are decorated in real gold and the body is pure white with gold edge and an additional gold line inside the border.

Raised Gold #220, cup and saucer, dates advertised 1930-40.

Raised Gold #221, bread and butter plate, 6½" in diameter, dates advertised 1930-40.

Raised Gold #222, tea plate, 7½" in diameter, dates advertised 1930-40.

Raised Gold #223, dinner plate, 9¾" in diameter, dates advertised 1930-40.

Raised Gold #224, fruit saucer, 5¼" in diameter, dates advertised 1930-40.

Raised Gold #225, soup plate, 7-1/8" in diameter, dates advertised 1930-40.

Raised Gold #226, platter, 9" x 12", dates advertised 1930-40.

Raised Gold #227, platter, 10¼" x 14", dates advertised 1930-40.

Raised Gold #228, casserole, 10¼" diameter, dates advertised 1930-34.

Raised Gold #229, open vegetable dish, 10½" across handles, dates advertised 1930-40.

Raised Gold #230, gravy boat, 8½" long, dates advertised 1930-40.

Raised Gold #231, handled relish dish, 5" x 7", dates advertised 1930-40.

Raised Gold #232, cake plate, 9¾" diameter, dates advertised 1930-40.

Raised Gold #233, salad bowl, 10" in diameter, dates advertised 1930-40.

Raised Gold #234, teapot, five cup size, 4½" tall, dates advertised 1930-36.

Raised Gold #235, sugar (3-5/8" tall) and cream (3-1/8" tall) set, dates advertised 1930-35.

Raised Gold #236, oatmeal dish, 5½" in diameter, dates advertised 1930-40.

Raised Gold #237, butter tub with drainer, 5-1/8" in diameter, dates advertised 1930-40.

Raised Gold #238, celery tray, 5¾" x 12", dates advertised 1930-40.

Raised Gold #239, salt and pepper shakers, 3" tall, dates advertised 1930-40.

Raised Gold #240, whipped cream set, 4½" bowl, dates advertised 1930-40.

Raised Gold #241, pickle set, 5½" diameter, dates advertised 1930-34.

Raised Gold #242, berry sugar (6½" tall) and cream (5¾" tall) set, dates advertised 1930-34.

Raised Gold #243, sugar (2½" tall) and cream (3½" tall) set, dates advertised 1930-34.

Raised Gold #244, teapot tile, 6" diameter, dates advertised 1930-39.

Raised Gold #245, divided relish dish, 8½" x 4¾", dates advertised 1930-39.

Raised Gold #246, comport, 6½" diameter, dates advertised 1930-35.

Raised Gold #296, breakfast plate, 8½" diameter, dates advertised 1930-40.

Raised Gold #297, open vegetable dish, 9¼" across handles, dates advertised 1930-40.

Raised Gold #298, individual salt and pepper shakers, 2-9/16" tall, dates advertised 1930-40.

Raised Gold #299, after dinner coffee pot, holds six cups, dates advertised 1930-39.

Raised Gold #300, after dinner coffee cup set, cups are 2-1/8" tall, dates advertised 1930-35.

Raised Gold #301, jam jar, 5″ tall with cover, dates advertised 1930-40.

Raised Gold #325, deep bowl, 5½″ diameter, dates advertised 1930-34.

Raised Gold #326, platter, 7½″ x 10¼″, dates advertised 1930-34.

Raised Gold #327, candy jar, 5″ tall, dates advertised 1930-39.

Raised Gold #333, bon bon dish, 6¼″ diameter, dates advertised 1930-40.

Raised Gold #362, cream soup cup, diameter 5-1/8″, dates advertised 1930-40.

Raised Gold #402, casserole, 10¼″ diameter, dates advertised 1935-40.

Raised Gold #437, sugar (3-5/8″ tall) and cream (3-1/8″ tall), dates advertised 1936-40.

Raised Gold #440, divided vegetable dish, 9½″ diameter, dates advertised 1936-40.

Raised Gold #443, teapot, five cup size, 4½″ tall, dates advertised 1936-39.

Raised Gold #451, sugar and cream set, 2¼″ tall, dates advertised 1937-40.

Raised Gold #454, celery tray, 4-3/8″ x 10″, dates advertised 1937-40.

The "Linden" pattern was offered in the 1935-40 catalogs and may possibly have been offered in 1941. All the items listed below were offered between the years of 1935 and 1940 except for #441 which was offered in the 1936-40 catalogs.

The body of the Linden pattern is clear white set off by a wide wavy background. The decoration is of a bouquet of pink roses and yellow and blue flowers connected by a scroll work in golden brown. This is touched off by a Chinese red border. All handles have heavy matt gold and the edges are covered with gold.

Linden #411, cup and saucer.

Linden #412, bread and butter plate, 6¼″ in diameter.

Linden #413, tea plate, 7½″ in diameter.

Linden #414, breakfast plate, 8-5/8″ in diameter.

Linden #415, dinner plate, 9¾″ in diameter.

Linden #416, fruit saucer, 5¼″ in diameter.

Linden #417, soup plate, 7-3/8″ in diameter.

Linden #418, cream soup (4½″ diameter) and plates (7-1/8″ diameter.)

Linden #419, fruit or salad plate (square), 7¾″ wide.

Linden #420, oatmeal, 5¾″ in diameter.

Linden #421, platter, 11¾″ x 8¾″.

Linden #422, platter, 13¾″ x 10¼″.

Linden #423, platter, 16″ x 12″.

Linden #424, deep bowl, 5-1/8″ in diameter.

Linden #425, open vegetable dish, 10½″ across handles.

Linden #426, open vegetable, 9″ across handles.

Linden #427, casserole, 10¼″ diameter.

Linden #428, gravy boat, 9″ long.

Linden #429, cake plate, 10½″ wide.

Linden #430, salad bowl, 10-3/8″ wide.

Linden #431, sugar (3-5/8″ tall) and cream set.

Linden #432, teapot, holds five cups.

Linden #433, celery tray, 12-7/8″ x 6¼″.

Linden #434, pickle dish, 8-5/8″ long.

Linden #435, butter dish, 7-3/8″ diameter.

Linden #436, salt and pepper shaker set, 4″ tall.

Linden #441, divided vegetable dish, 9½″ diameter, dates advertised 1936-40.

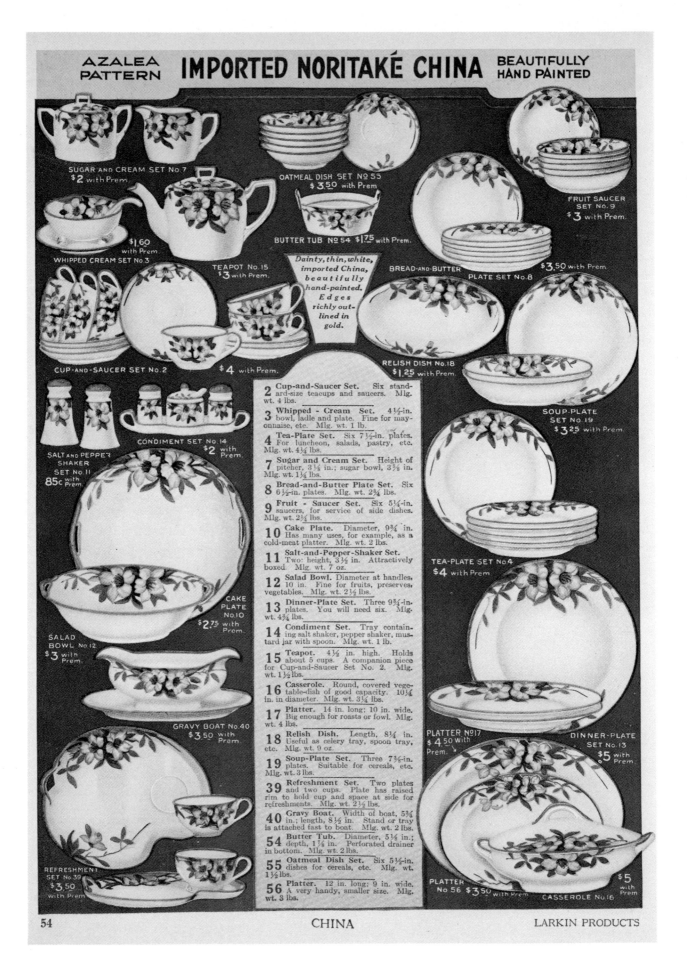

AZALEA PATTERN

IMPORTED NORITAKÉ CHINA

BEAUTIFULLY HAND PAINTED

SUGAR AND CREAM SET No.7
$2 with Prem.

OATMEAL DISH SET NO.55
$3.50 with Prem

FRUIT SAUCER SET No.9
$3 with Prem.

WHIPPED CREAM SET No.3
$1.60 with Prem.

TEAPOT No.15
$3 with Prem.

BUTTER TUB No.54 $1.75 with Prem.

Dainty, thin, white, imported China, beautifully hand-painted. Edges richly outlined in gold.

BREAD-AND-BUTTER PLATE SET No.8
$3.50 with Prem

CUP-AND-SAUCER SET No.2
$4 with Prem.

RELISH DISH No.18
$1.25 with Prem.

SOUP-PLATE SET No.19
$3.25 with Prem.

SALT AND PEPPER SHAKER SET No.11
85c with Prem.

CONDIMENT SET No.14
$2 with Prem.

CAKE PLATE No.10
$2.75 with Prem.

SALAD BOWL No.12
$3 with Prem.

GRAVY BOAT No.40
$3.50 with Prem.

REFRESHMENT SET No.39
$3.50 with Prem

TEA-PLATE SET No.4
$4 with Prem

PLATTER No.17
$4.50 with Prem

DINNER-PLATE SET No.13
$5 with Prem

PLATTER No.56 $3.50 with Prem

CASSEROLE No.16 $5 with Prem

2 Cup-and-Saucer Set. Six standard-size teacups and saucers. Mlg. wt. 4 lbs.

3 Whipped - Cream Set. 4½-in. bowl, ladle and plate. Fine for mayonnaise, etc. Mlg. wt. 1 lb.

4 Tea-Plate Set. Six 7½-in. plates. For luncheon, salads, pastry, etc. Mlg. wt. 4¼ lbs.

7 Sugar and Cream Set. Height of pitcher, 3⅛ in.; sugar bowl, 3⅝ in. Mlg. wt. 1¼ lbs.

8 Bread-and-Butter Plate Set. Six 6½-in. plates. Mlg. wt. 2¾ lbs.

9 Fruit - Saucer Set. Six 5¼-in. saucers, for service of side dishes. Mlg. wt. 2¼ lbs.

10 Cake Plate. Diameter, 9¾ in. Has many uses, for example, as a cold-meat platter. Mlg. wt. 2 lbs.

11 Salt-and-Pepper-Shaker Set. Two; height, 3½ in. Attractively boxed. Mlg. wt. 7 oz.

12 Salad Bowl. Diameter at handles, 10 in. Fine for fruits, preserves, vegetables. Mlg. wt. 2½ lbs.

13 Dinner-Plate Set. Three 9¾-in. plates. You will need six. Mlg. wt. 4¾ lbs.

14 Condiment Set. Tray containing salt shaker, pepper shaker, mustard jar with spoon. Mlg. wt. 1 lb.

15 Teapot. 4½ in. high. Holds about 5 cups. A companion piece for Cup-and-Saucer Set No. 2. Mlg. wt. 1½ lbs.

16 Casserole. Round, covered vegetable-dish of good capacity. 10¼ in. in diameter. Mlg. wt. 3¼ lbs.

17 Platter. 14 in. long; 10 in. wide. Big enough for roasts or fowl. Mlg. wt. 4 lbs.

18 Relish Dish. Length, 8¼ in. Useful as celery tray, spoon tray, etc. Mlg. wt. 9 oz.

19 Soup-Plate Set. Three 7⅜-in. plates. Suitable for cereals, etc. Mlg. wt. 3 lbs.

39 Refreshment Set. Two plates and two cups. Plate has raised rim to hold cup and space at side for refreshments. Mlg. wt. 2½ lbs.

40 Gravy Boat. Width of boat, 5¾ in.; length, 8½ in. Stand or tray is attached fast to boat. Mlg. wt. 2 lbs.

54 Butter Tub. Diameter, 5⅛ in.; depth, 1⅞ in. Perforated drainer in bottom. Mlg. wt. 2 lbs.

55 Oatmeal Dish Set. Six 5½-in. dishes for cereals, etc. Mlg. wt. 1½ lbs.

56 Platter. 12 in. long; 9 in. wide. A very handy, smaller size. Mlg. wt. 3 lbs.

Larkin Catalog #97 Spring & Summer 1927.

38

Larkin Catalog #105 Spring/Summer 1931.

AZALEA CHINA OPPOSITE

Dainty, thin, white, imported China, beautifully hand-painted. Edges and handles traced in gold.

2 ***Cup-and-Saucer Set. $4 with PREM.*** Six standard-size teacups and saucers. Mlg. wt. 4 lbs.

3 ***Whipped-Cream Set. $1.60 with PREM.*** 4½-in. bowl, ladle, plate. Fine for mayonnaise. Mailing weight 1 lb.

4 ***Tea-Plate Set. $4 with PREM.*** Six 7½-in. plates. For luncheon, salads, pastry. Mlg. wt. 4½ lbs.

7 ***Sugar and Cream Set. $2 with PREM.*** Height of pitcher, 3⅛ in.; bowl, 3⅝ in. Mlg. wt. 1½ lbs.

8 ***Bread-and-Butter Plate Set. $3.50 with PREM.*** Six 6½-in. plates. Mailing weight 3 lbs.

9 ***Fruit-Saucer Set. $3 with PREM.*** Six 5¼-in. saucers. Mailing weight 2¼ lbs.

10 ***Cake Plate. $2.50 with PREM.*** Diameter, 9¾ in. Fine for cold meat. Mlg. wt. 2 lbs.

12 ***Salad Bowl. $2.75 with PREM.*** Diameter, 10 in. Mailing weight 2¼ lbs.

13 ***Dinner-Plate Set. $5 with PREM.*** THREE 9¾-in. plates. Mlg. wt. 4½ lbs.

14 ***Condiment Set. $2 with PREM.*** Tray, salt shaker, pepper shaker, mustard jar, spoon. Mailing weight 1 lb.

15 ***Teapot. $3 with PREM.*** 4½ in. high. Holds 5 cups. Mailing weight 1¾ lbs.

16 ***Casserole. $5 with PREM.*** Round, covered vegetable-dish. Diam., 10¼ in. Mlg.wt. 3½ lbs.

17 ***Platter. $4.50 with PREM.*** 14 x 10¼ in. Mlg. wt. 3¾ lbs.

19 ***Soup-Plate Set. $3.25 with PREM.*** THREE 7⅛-in. plates. Mailing weight 3 lbs.

39 ***Refreshment Set. $3.30 with PREM.*** Two plates, two cups. Raised rim holds cup. Mailing weight 2 lbs.

40 ***Gravy Boat. $3.50 with PREM.*** Width of boat, 5¾ in.; length, 8½ in. Stand attached. Mailing weight 1¾ lbs.

54 ***Butter Tub. $1.75 with PREM.*** Diam., 5⅛ in.; depth, 1⅞ in. Drainer. Mlg. wt. 1¼ lbs.

55 ***Oatmeal Dish Set. $3.50 with PREM.*** Six 5½-in. dishes. Mailing weight 3¼ lbs.

56 ***Platter. $3.50 with PREM.*** 12 x 9. Mlg. wt. 2¼ lbs.

89 ***Salt and Pepper Shaker Set. 70c with PREM.*** 3 in. high. Gold tops. Mlg. wt. 5 oz.

97 ***Syrup Pitcher. $2.25 with PREM.*** 4½ in. high with cover; plate, 5½ in. diam. Mailing weight 1½ lbs.

98 ***Breakfast Plate. $4 with PREM.*** THREE 8½-in. plates. Mailing weight 3¼ lbs.

99 ***Celery or Roll Tray. $3 with PREM.*** 12 x 5¾ in. Mailing weight 1¾ lbs.

100 ***Jug. $2.75 with PREM.*** Holds 1 qt. 5⅝ in. high. Mailing weight 1¾ lbs.

101 ***Open Vegetable Dish. $3.25 with PREM.*** 10½ in. long across handles. Mlg. wt. 2 lbs.

119 ***Relish Dish. $2.75 with PREM.*** 10 in. diam. Mailing weight 2 lbs.

120 ***Egg Cup Set. $1.50 with PREM.*** Four cups, 3⅛ in. high, for soft-boiled eggs. Mailing weight 1¼ lbs.

121 ***Pickle or Lemon Set. $1 with PREM.*** Dainty handled plate, 5½ in. diameter. Bone fork, 4¾ in. long, decorated. Mailing weight 9 oz.

122 ***Berry, Sugar and Cream Set. $2 with PREM.*** Also for sugar and syrup for waffles. Sugar shaker 6½ in. high; cream pitcher, 5¾ in. Mlg. wt. 1¼ lbs.

123 ***Sugar and Cream Set. $2 with PREM.*** Cream pitcher, 3½ in. high; sugar bowl, 2½ in. Mailing weight 10 oz.

124 ***Bouillon Cups and Saucers. $5 with PREM.*** Set of Six. Smart two-handled cups for consomme or soup. Saucers, 5½ in. in diameter; cups, 3½ in. Mailing weight 4 lbs.

125 ***Jam Jar. $2.50 with PREM.*** For jam, honey, etc. Plate, 5¼ in. in diameter. Jar, 5 in. high. Ladle, 4¼ in. Mlg. wt. 1½ lbs.

126 ***Individual Salt and Pepper Shakers. $1 with PREM.*** Set of four. Two salt, two pepper shakers, 2 9/16 in. high. Mailing weight 6 oz.

169 ***Teapot Tile. 90c with PREM.*** Protects table from heat of teapot or coffee pot. Diam., 6 in. Mailing weight 12 oz.

170 ***Comport. $2 with PREM.*** Graceful piece of many uses. 6½ in. diam.; 2¾ in. high. Mailing weight 1¼ lbs.

171 ***Two-Compartment Relish Dish. $2 with PREM.*** 8¼ in. long; 4¾ in. wide. Mailing weight 1 lb.

172 ***Vegetable Dish. $2.50 with PREM.*** Convenient smaller size, 9¼ in. across handles; 6¾ in. wide. Mailing weight 1¼ lbs.

182 ***After Dinner Coffee Pot. $2 with PREM.*** Capacity, 6 cups of after-dinner size. Mailing weight 1¼ lbs.

183 ***After Dinner Cup & Saucer Set. $3.60 with PREM.*** SIX dainty little cups, 2⅛ in. high. Saucers, 4¼ in. in diameter. Mailing weight 2½ lbs.

184 ***Bonbon Dish. $1 with PREM.*** Charming Dish for candies, nuts, etc. Diameter, 6¼ in. Mailing weight 13 oz.

185 ***Grapefruit or Candy Bowl. $1.50 with PREM.*** Unique new Bowl for varied purposes. Diameter, 4½ in.; height, 3½ in. Mailing weight 13 oz.

186 ***Platter. $8 with PREM.*** Extra large. For big roasts and fowl. 16 x 12 in. Mlg. wt. 5⅔ lbs.

187 ***Footed Vase. $1.50 with PREM.*** Attractive fan shape. Height, 5½ in. Mlg. wt. 13 oz.

188 ***Nut or Fruit Bowl, $3 with PREM.*** Oddly fashioned in shell shape. 7¾ in. long. Mailing weight 1¾ lbs.

189 ***Spoon Holder. $1.50 with PREM.*** Can also be used for cube sugar. 6¼ in. long without handles. 8 in. long over all. 1¾ in. wide. Mailing weight 12 oz.

190 ***Vinegar Bottle. $1.50 with PREM.*** Handled. For either oil or vinegar. 6¼ in. high to top of stopper. Mlg. wt. 10 oz.

191 ***Handled Mustard Jar with Spoon. 60c with PREM.*** Jar, 2¾ in. in diameter, 1⅞ in. high. Mailing weight 7 oz.

192 ***Match or Toothpick Holder. 50c with PREM.*** 2½ in. high. Diameter, 1¾ in. Mailing weight 3 oz.

193 ***Dolly Varden Basket. 70c with PREM.*** Distinctively shaped. 4⅜ in. long; 2½ in. wide; 4 in. high to top of handle. Mailing weight 7 oz.

194 ***Relish Dish. $1.20 with PREM.*** Length, 8¼ in. Useful as celery tray, spoon tray. Mailing weight 14 oz.

310 ***Deep Bowl. $1.50 with PREM.*** Handy size. 5⅛ in. in diameter; 2⅞ in. high. Mailing weight 1 lb.

311 ***Platter. $2.75 with PREM.*** New small size 10¼ x 7½ in. Mailing weight 1½ lbs.

312 ***Butter Chips. $1.35 with PREM.*** Six. 3¼ in. in diameter. Mailing weight ¾ lb.

313 ***Covered Candy Jar. $2.50 with PREM.*** Smartly shaped. 4 in. in diameter; about 5 in. high over all. Mlg. wt. 1¼ lbs.

314 ***Cheese or Butter Dish. $2 with PREM.*** Plate, 6½ in. in diameter; cover, 5 in. in diameter; 1½ in. high. Mlg. wt. 1½ lbs.

315 ***Fruit or Salad Plate Set. $3.50 with PREM.*** Oddly styled. THREE 7⅝ in. in diameter. Mailing weight 2¾ lbs.

338 ***Grill Plates. $5 with PREM.*** Set of two plates, 10¼ in. in diameter, that permit serving of meat and two vegetables on one plate. Mlg. wt. 3 lbs.

Desriptions for Catalog #105 Spring & Summer 1931.

HAND PAINTED NORITAKE

PATTERN EXCLUSIVE WITH LARKIN CO INC.

This lovely Azalea Pattern in Noritaké China has been the choice of thousands. It is by all odds our most popular pattern, preferred for its beauty, richness and big value. You will delight in its charm. The pink azaleas are hand painted in their natural beauty! They stand out prettily against the clear whiteness of the body. The gold tracing on edges and handles adds the final touch of smartness.

No picture or description, however, can tell you how delightful and desirable this china actually is. Its delicate coloring and its thinness, such as only genuine china possesses, combine to make it unbelievably dainty. Design and decoration, too, make it a delightful pattern for dinner service, or a tea or luncheon set.

Best of all, Noritaké China sells at remarkably low prices. All patterns are exclusive with Larkin Co. Nowhere else can you get this lovely china, which means that you won't see these patterns on bargain counters.

Accumulate a few pieces at a time to make up a set of just the size and variety you require. You can feel free to do this because Noritaké China is made by one of the largest and best-known manufacturers of fine china.

2 **Cup-and-Saucer Set. *With Prem.* $4.00, *Cash Price* $2.00.** Six standard-size teacups and saucers. Mlg. wt. 3½ lbs.

4 **Tea Plate Set. *With Prem.* $4.00, *Cash Price* $2.00.** Six 7½-in. plates. For luncheon, salads, pastry. Mlg. wt. 4½ lbs.

8 **Bread-and-Butter Plate Set. *With Prem.* $3.40, *Cash Price* $1.70.** Six 6½-in. plates. Mailing weight 3 lbs.

9 **Fruit Saucer Set. *With Prem.* $3.40, *Cash Price* $1.70.** Six 5¼-in. saucers for fruit, sauce, etc. Mailing weight 2¼ lbs.

10 **Cake Plate. *With Prem.* $2.40, *Cash Price* $1.20.** Diameter, 9¾ in. Fine for cold meat. Mlg. wt. 2 lbs.

12 **Salad Bowl. *With Prem.* $2.80, *Cash Price* $1.40.** Diameter, 10 in. Mlg. wt. 2¼ lbs.

13 **Dinner Plate Set. *With Prem.* $5.00, *Cash Price* $2.50.** THREE 9¾-in. plates. Mlg. wt. 4 lbs.

17 **Platter. *With Prem.* $5.60, *Cash Price* $2.80.** Large size, 14 x 10¼ in. for roasts and fowl. Mlg. wt. 3¾ lbs.

19 **Soup Plate Set. *With Prem.* $3.70, *Cash Price* $1.85.** THREE 7⅛-in. plates. Mlg. wt. 3 lbs.

39 **Refreshment Set. *With Prem.* $3.10, *Cash Price* $1.55.** Two plates, two cups. Rim holds cup. Mlg. wt. 1¼ lbs.

40 **Gravy Boat. *With Prem.* $3.60, *Cash Price* $1.80.** Width of boat, 5¾ in.; length, 8½ in. Stand attached. Mlg. wt. 1¾ lbs.

55 **Oatmeal Dish Set. *With Prem.* $3.50, *Cash Price* $1.75.** Six 5¾-in. dishes. Mlg. wt. 3 lbs.

56 **Platter. *With Prem.* $4.00, *Cash Price* $2.00.** 12 x 9 in. Mlg. wt. 2¼ lbs.

89 **Salt and Pepper Shaker Set. *With Prem.* 60c, *Cash Price* 30c.** 3 in. high. Gold tops. Mlg. wt. 5 oz.

98 **Breakfast Plates. *With Prem.* $3.70, *Cash Price* $1.85.** THREE 8½-in. plates. Mlg. wt. 3¼ lbs.

99 **Celery or Roll Tray. *With Prem.* $2.90, *Cash Price* $1.45.** 12 x 5¾ in. Mlg. wt. 1¾ lbs.

101 **Open Vegetable Dish. *With Prem.* $3.40, *Cash Price* $1.70.** 10½ in. across handles. Mlg. wt. 1½ lbs.

121 **Lemon Set. *With Prem.* 90c, *Cash Price* 45c.** Dainty, handled plate, 5½ in. in diameter. Bone pick 4¾ in. long, decorated. Mlg. wt. 10 oz.

124 **Bouillon Cups and Saucers. *With Prem.* $5.70, *Cash Price* $2.85.** Set of six. Smart, two-handled cups for consomme or soup. Saucers, 5½ in. diam.; cups, 3½ in. Mlg. wt. 4 lbs.

169 **Teapot Tile. *With Prem.* $1.00, *Cash Price* 50c.** Protects table from heat of teapot or coffee pot. Diameter 6 in. Mlg. wt. 12 oz.

172 **Vegetable Dish. *With Prem.* $2.80, *Cash Price* $1.40.** Convenient smaller size, 9¼ in. across handles; 6¾ in. wide. Mlg. wt. 1¼ lbs.

186 **Platter. *With Prem.* $9.00, *Cash Price* $4.50.** Extra large. For big roasts, turkey and fowl. 16 x 12 in. Mlg. wt. 5¾ lbs.

194 **Relish Dish. *With Prem.* $1.20, *Cash Price* 60c.** Length, 7⅛ in. Useful as celery tray, spoon tray. Mlg. wt. 10 oz.

310 **Deep Bowl. *With Prem.* $1.50, *Cash Price* 75c.** Handy size, 5⅛ in. in diameter; 2⅞ in. high. Mlg. wt. 1 lb.

314 **Cheese or Butter Dish. *With Prem.* $2.10, *Cash Price* $1.05.** Plate, 6½ in. in diameter; cover, 5 in. in diameter; 1½ in. high. Mlg. wt. 1½ lbs.

315 **Fruit or Salad Plate Set. *With Prem.* $4.00, *Cash Price* $2.00.** Oddly styled. THREE 7⅝ in. in diameter. Mlg. wt. 2¾ lbs.

363 **Cream Soup Set. *With Prem.* $5.60, *Cash Price* $2.80.** THREE smart cups for cream soup, grapefruit, baked apples, etc. 5⅛-in. in diameter. Use with Tea Plates No. 4 or Salad Plates No. 315. Mlg. wt. 1½ lbs.

372 **Casserole. *With Prem.* $5.60, *Cash Price* $2.80.** Round covered vegetable dish. Diameter, 10¾ in. Mlg. wt. 3 lbs.

400 **Teapot. *With Prem.* $2.80, *Cash Price* $1.40.** 4½ in. high. Holds 5 cups. Mlg. wt. 1½ lbs.

401 **Sugar and Cream Set. *With Prem.* $2.40, *Cash Price* $1.20.** Height of pitcher, 3⅛ in.; bowl, 3⅝ in. Mlg. wt. 1½ lbs.

439 **Divided Vegetable Dish. *With Prem.* $4.00, *Cash Price* $2.00.** Delightfully convenient. Partition permits serving two vegetables in the one dish. 9½ in. in diameter. Mlg. wt. 2 lbs.

444 **Celery Tray. *With Prem.* $1.70, *Cash Price* 85c.** For dwarf celery, relishes, etc. 10 in. long. 4⅜ in. wide. Mlg. wt. 1 lb.

449 **Sugar and Creamer Set. *With Prem.* $1.70, *Cash Price* 85c.** Dainty new pieces of charming design. About 2¼ in. high. Mlg. wt. 1 lb.

450 **Twin Relish Dish. *With Prem.* $1.70, *Cash Price* 85c.** Convenient new dish for serving two relishes. 7½ in. long. Gold handled. Mlg. wt. 12 oz.

452 **Vase. *With Prem.* $2.30, *Cash Price* $1.15.** Charming new vase of smart design and good size. 6¼ in. high. Mlg. wt. 8 oz.

453 **Mayonnaise Set. *With Prem.* $2.20, *Cash Price* $1.10.** Also for whipped cream, jelly, etc. Plate, 6¾ in. diam.; bowl, 5½ in. Ladle. Mlg. wt. 1 lb.

Descriptions for Catalog #119 Spring & Summer 1938.

Larkin Catalog #119 Spring/Summer 1938.

41

POPULAR SCENIC PATTERN
IMPORTED NORITAKE' CHINA

Beauty! Charm! Richness! All these are found in this lovely Scenic pattern. No wonder it is popular! It is just as lovely as it looks—dainty and thin and wonderfully hand-painted with a scenic design of great attractiveness, in rich autumn colors, brown predominating. Various offers can be combined to form a dinner set, a tea set, a berry set or a cake set. And the gayly-colored individual pieces add a delightful touch to your table!

41 Teapot. $2.70 with PREMIUM. 5-cup capacity; 4½ in. high. Mlg. wt. 1¾ lbs.

42 Sugar and Creamer. $1.60 with PREMIUM. Height, pitcher, 3½ in. Mlg. wt. 1½ lbs.

43 Cup-and-Saucer Set. $3.50 with PREMIUM. Six standard-size teacups and saucers. Mlg. wt. 4 lbs.

44 Tea Plate Set. $3.50 with PREMIUM. Six 7½-in. plates. Mlg. wt. 4½ lbs.

45 Cake Plate. $2 with PREMIUM. Diameter, 9¾ in. Mlg. wt. 2 lbs.

46 Bread-and-Butter Plate Set. $2.80 with PREMIUM. Six 6½-in. plates. Mlg. wt. 3 lbs.

47 Salad Bowl. $2.40 with PREMIUM. Diameter, 10 in. Mlg. wt. 2¼ lbs.

48 Fruit Saucer Set. $2.80 with PREMIUM. Six saucers. Diameter, 5¼ in. Mlg. wt. 2¼ lbs.

49 Condiment Set. $1.80 with PREMIUM. Tray, salt shaker, pepper shaker, mustard jar, spoon. Mlg. wt. 13 oz.

111 Breakfast Plate Set. $3.20 with PREMIUM. THREE 8½-in. plates. Mlg. wt. 3½ lbs.

113 Platter. $3.30 with PREMIUM. Medium size, 12 in. long. Mlg. wt. 2½ lbs.

114 Open Vegetable Dish. $2.80 with PREMIUM. 10½ in. long. 7¾ in. wide. Mlg. wt. 2 lbs.

135 Pickle Set. $1 with PREMIUM. Handled plate, 5½ in. in diameter; 4¾-in. bone fork. Mlg. wt. 10 oz.

A score or more of delightful gifts are found in the charming individual pieces.

China as lovely as this will satisfy the most fastidious. It is imported ware, pleasingly thin and beautifully hand-painted. You will like it!

Get a few pieces at a time. Soon you will have a lovely tea set with just the variety and number of pieces that you require.

136 Jam Jar. $2.50 with PREMIUM. Jar, 5 in. high with cover. 5¼-in. plate; 4¾-in. ladle. Mlg. wt. 1½ lbs.

137 Salt and Pepper Shakers. 50c with PREMIUM. Height, 3 in. Mlg. wt. 6 oz.

138 Berry Sugar and Cream Set. $2 with PREMIUM. Sugar shaker, 6½ in. high; pitcher, 5¾ in. Mlg. wt. 1¼ lbs.

175 Comport. $2 with PREMIUM. 6½ in. in diameter; 2¾ in. high. Mlg. wt. 1¼ lbs.

176 Compartment Relish Dish. $2 with PREMIUM. 8¼ in. long; 4¾ in. wide. Mlg. wt. 1 lb.

179 After-Dinner Coffee Pot. $2 with PREMIUM. Capacity, six cups of after-dinner size. Mlg. wt. 1¼ lbs.

201 Dinner Plate Set. $4.50 with PREMIUM. THREE 9¾-in. plates. Mlg. wt. 4½ lbs.

202 Platter. $4.50 with PREMIUM. Large size, 14 x 10¼ in. Mlg. wt. 4 lbs.

203 Oatmeal Dishes. $3 with PREMIUM. Six 5¾-in. dishes. Mlg. wt. 3¼ lbs.

206 Whipped Cream Set. $1.60 with PREMIUM. 4½-in. bowl, ladle and plate. For mayonnaise, also. Mlg. wt. 1 lb.

207 Celery Tray. $2.25 with PREMIUM. Size, 12 x 5¾ in. Mlg. wt. 1¾ lbs.

208 Individual Salt and Pepper Shakers. 80c with PREMIUM. Set of 4. Two salt, two pepper shakers. 2⁹⁄₁₆ in. high. Mlg. wt. 6 oz.

209 Footed Vase. $1.50 with PREMIUM. Top opening, 4 x 1½ in. Height, 5½ in. Very gracefully shaped. Mlg. wt. 13 oz.

214 Casserole. $4.50 with PREMIUM. Round, covered vegetable dish. Diameter, 10¼ in. Mlg. wt. 3¼ lbs.

215 Gravy Boat. $3 with PREMIUM. Width of boat, 5¾ in.; length, 8½ in. Fast stand. Mlg. wt. 2 lbs.

216 Soup Plates. $3 with PREMIUM. Set of THREE 7½-in. plates. Mlg. wt. 3 lbs.

317 Platter. $2.75 with PREMIUM. Small size, for cold meats. 10¼ in. x 7½ in. Mlg. wt. 1½ lbs.

318 Candy Jar. $2.50 with PREMIUM. Diameter, 4 in.; height, 5 in. Mlg. wt. 1¼ lbs.

319 Vinegar and Oil Set. $1.75 with PREMIUM. Two bottles, 6½ in. tip to tip, conveniently joined together. Mlg. wt. 1 lb.

320 Cheese or Butter Dish. $1.80 with PREMIUM. Diameter of plate, 6½ in.; cover, 5 in. Height, 1½ in. Mlg. wt. 1½ lbs.

323 Fruit or Salad Plate Set. $3.50 with PREMIUM. THREE 7⅝-in. plates. Mlg. wt. 2¾ lbs.

324 Celery and Relish Dish. $2.25 with PREMIUM. 11½ in. x 6 in. Mlg. wt. 2 lbs.

48 *Larkin Co Inc.*

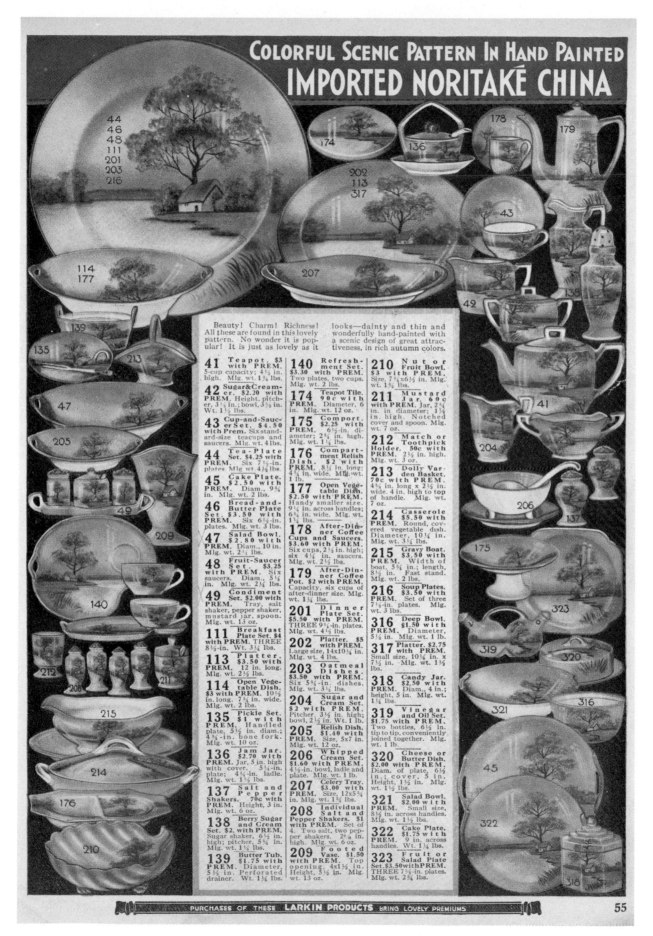

Larkin Catalog #104 Fall/Winter 1930.

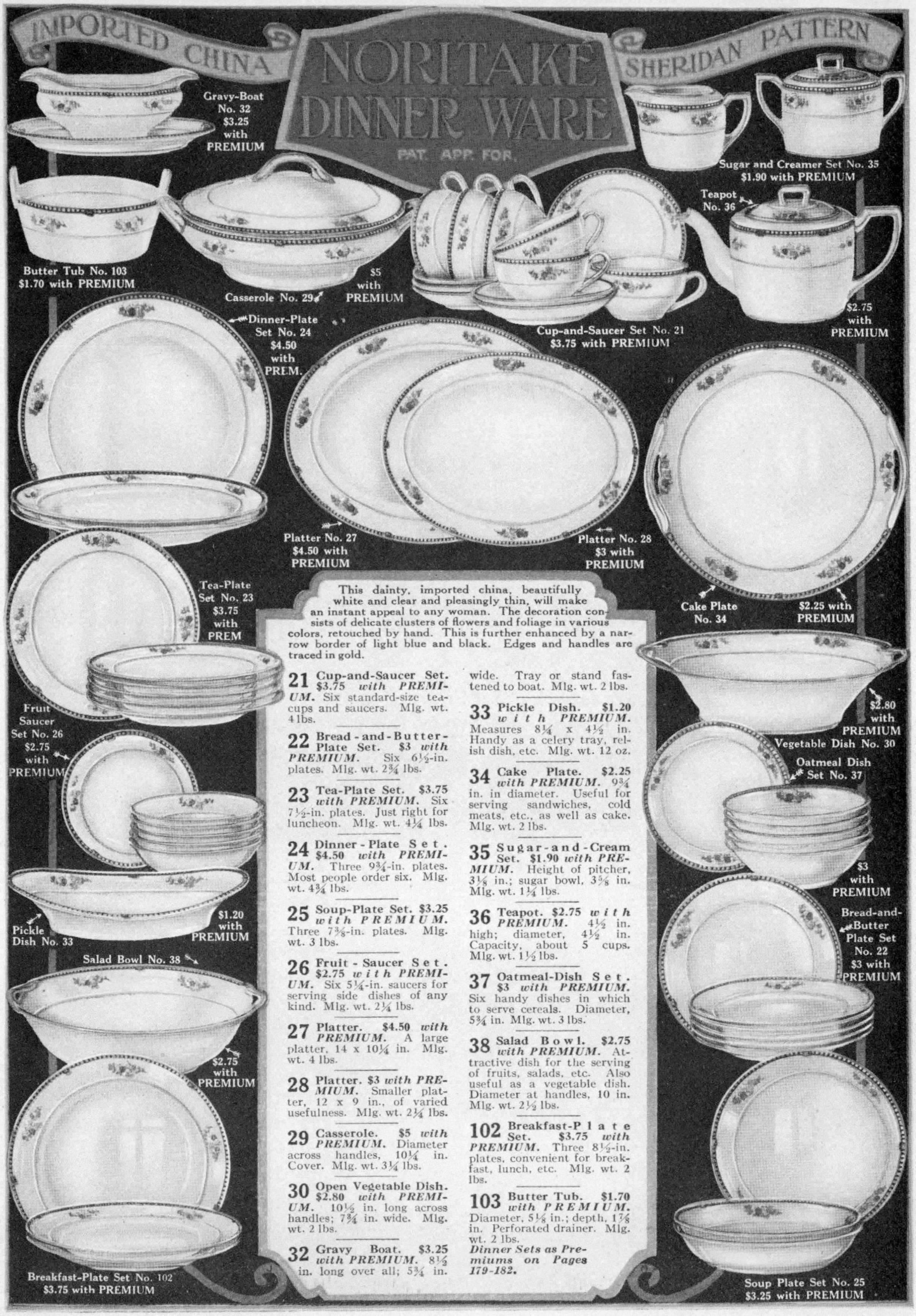
IMPORTED CHINA
NORITAKE DINNER WARE
PAT. APP. FOR.
SHERIDAN PATTERN
Gravy-Boat No. 32 $3.25 with PREMIUM
Sugar and Creamer Set No. 35 $1.90 with PREMIUM
Teapot No. 36
$2.75 with PREMIUM
Butter Tub No. 103 $1.70 with PREMIUM
Casserole No. 29 $5 with PREMIUM
Cup-and-Saucer Set No. 21 $3.75 with PREMIUM
Dinner-Plate Set No. 24 $4.50 with PREM.
Platter No. 27 $4.50 with PREMIUM
Platter No. 28 $3 with PREMIUM
Cake Plate No. 34
$2.25 with PREMIUM
Tea-Plate Set No. 23 $3.75 with PREM
Fruit Saucer Set No. 26 $2.75 with PREMIUM
$2.80 with PREMIUM
Vegetable Dish No. 30
Oatmeal Dish Set No. 37
$3 with PREMIUM
Pickle Dish No. 33
$1.20 with PREMIUM
Salad Bowl No. 38
$2.75 with PREMIUM
Bread-and-Butter Plate Set No. 22 $3 with PREMIUM
Breakfast-Plate Set No. 102 $3.75 with PREMIUM
Soup Plate Set No. 25 $3.25 with PREMIUM

This dainty, imported china, beautifully white and clear and pleasingly thin, will make an instant appeal to any woman. The decoration consists of delicate clusters of flowers and foliage in various colors, retouched by hand. This is further enhanced by a narrow border of light blue and black. Edges and handles are traced in gold.

21 Cup-and-Saucer Set. $3.75 *with PREMIUM.* Six standard-size teacups and saucers. Mlg. wt. 4 lbs.

22 Bread-and-Butter-Plate Set. $3 *with PREMIUM.* Six 6½-in. plates. Mlg. wt. 2¾ lbs.

23 Tea-Plate Set. $3.75 *with PREMIUM.* Six 7½-in. plates. Just right for luncheon. Mlg. wt. 4¼ lbs.

24 Dinner-Plate Set. $4.50 *with PREMIUM.* Three 9¾-in. plates. Most people order six. Mlg. wt. 4¾ lbs.

25 Soup-Plate Set. $3.25 *with PREMIUM.* Three 7⅜-in. plates. Mlg. wt. 3 lbs.

26 Fruit-Saucer Set. $2.75 *with PREMIUM.* Six 5¼-in. saucers for serving side dishes of any kind. Mlg. wt. 2¼ lbs.

27 Platter. $4.50 *with PREMIUM.* A large platter, 14 x 10¼ in. Mlg. wt. 4 lbs.

28 Platter. $3 *with PREMIUM.* Smaller platter, 12 x 9 in., of varied usefulness. Mlg. wt. 2¼ lbs.

29 Casserole. $5 *with PREMIUM.* Diameter across handles, 10¼ in. Cover. Mlg. wt. 3¼ lbs.

30 Open Vegetable Dish. $2.80 *with PREMIUM.* 10½ in. long across handles; 7¾ in. wide. Mlg. wt. 2 lbs.

32 Gravy Boat. $3.25 *with PREMIUM.* 8½ in. long over all; 5¾ in. wide. Tray or stand fastened to boat. Mlg. wt. 2 lbs.

33 Pickle Dish. $1.20 *with PREMIUM.* Measures 8¼ x 4½ in. Handy as a celery tray, relish dish, etc. Mlg. wt. 12 oz.

34 Cake Plate. $2.25 *with PREMIUM.* 9¾ in. in diameter. Useful for serving sandwiches, cold meats, etc., as well as cake. Mlg. wt. 2 lbs.

35 Sugar-and-Cream Set. $1.90 *with PREMIUM.* Height of pitcher, 3⅛ in.; sugar bowl, 3⅝ in. Mlg. wt. 1¼ lbs.

36 Teapot. $2.75 *with PREMIUM.* 4½ in. high; diameter, 4½ in. Capacity, about 5 cups. Mlg. wt. 1½ lbs.

37 Oatmeal-Dish Set. $3 *with PREMIUM.* Six handy dishes in which to serve cereals. Diameter, 5¾ in. Mlg. wt. 3 lbs.

38 Salad Bowl. $2.75 *with PREMIUM.* Attractive dish for the serving of fruits, salads, etc. Also useful as a vegetable dish. Diameter at handles, 10 in. Mlg. wt. 2½ lbs.

102 Breakfast-Plate Set. $3.75 *with PREMIUM.* Three 8½-in. plates, convenient for breakfast, lunch, etc. Mlg. wt. 2 lbs.

103 Butter Tub. $1.70 *with PREMIUM.* Diameter, 5⅛ in.; depth, 1⅞ in. Perforated drainer. Mlg. wt. 2 lbs.

Dinner Sets as Premiums on Pages 179-182.

54 CHINA LARKIN PRODUCTS

Larkin Catalog #99 Spring/Summer 1928.

Beauty and Big Value!

THAT'S THE APPEAL of SHERIDAN PATTERN

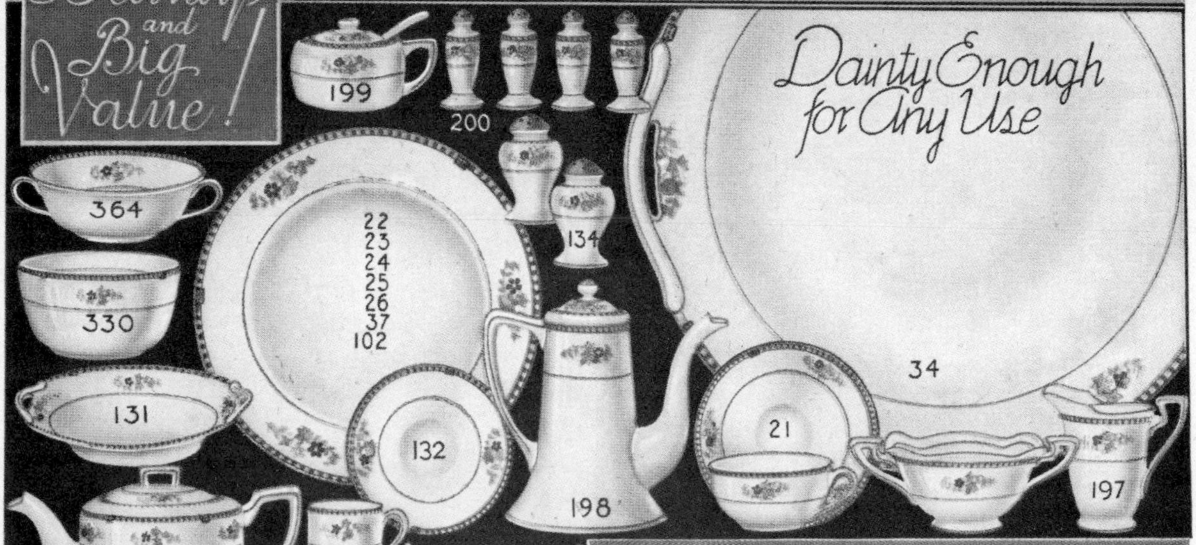

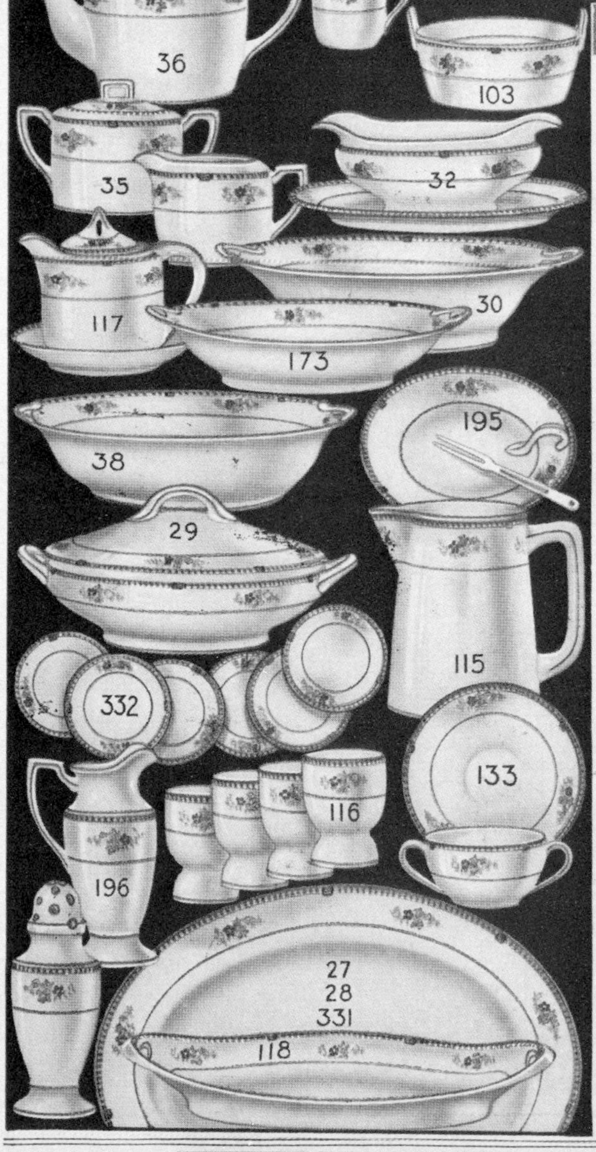

IMPORTED NORITAKE CHINA

The charm of this lovely Sheridan pattern—so appropriate for dinnerware—is the secret of its popularity. It's a great value, too. Dainty, imported china, beautifully white and clear and pleasingly thin, it is smart enough for any occasion. The decoration of delicate clusters of flowers and foliage in various colors, retouched by hand, is particularly suited as a dinnerware design. Narrow border of light blue and black. Gold-traced edges and handles.

21 Cup-and-Saucer Set. $3.75 **with PREMIUM.** Six standard cups, saucers. Mlg. wt. 4 lbs.

22 Bread-and-Butter Plate Set. $3 **with PREMIUM.** Six 6½-in. plates. Mlg. wt. 2¾ lbs.

23 Tea Plate Set. $3.75 **with PREMIUM.** Six 7½-in. plates. Mlg. wt. 4¼ lbs.

24 Dinner Plate Set. $4.50 **with PREMIUM.** THREE 9¾-in. plates. Mlg. wt. 4½ lbs.

25 Soup Plate Set. $3.25 **with PREMIUM.** THREE 7⅜-in. plates. Mlg. wt. 3 lbs.

26 Fruit Saucer Set. $2.75 **with PREMIUM.** Six 5¼-in. saucers for side dishes. Mlg. wt. 2¼ lbs.

27 Platter. $4.50 **with PREMIUM.** Large, 14 x 10¼ in. Mlg. wt. 4 lbs.

28 Platter. $3 **with PREMIUM.** Medium platter. 12 x 9 in. Mlg. wt. 2¼ lbs.

29 Casserole. $5 **with PREMIUM.** Round, covered vegetable dish, 10¼ in. across handles. Mlg. wt. 3¼ lbs.

30 Large Open Vegetable Dish. $2.80 **with PREMIUM.** 10½ in. long across handles; 7¾ in. wide. Wt. 2 lbs.

32 Gravy Boat. $3.25 **with PREMIUM.** 8½ in. long; 5¾ in. wide. Fast tray. Wt. 2 lbs.

34 Cake Plate. $2.25 **with PREMIUM.** 9¾ in. wide. Wt. 1¾ lbs.

35 Sugar and Cream Set. $1.90 **with PREMIUM.** Height, pitcher, 3⅜ in.; sugar bowl, 3⅝ in. Mlg. wt. 1¼ lbs.

36 Teapot. $2.75 **with PREMIUM.** 4½ in. high. Capacity, about 5 cups. Mlg wt 1¾ lbs.

37 Oatmeal Dish Set. $3 **with PREM.** Six dishes. Diameter, 5¾ in. Mlg. wt. 3¼ lbs.

38 Salad Bowl. $2.75 **with PREMIUM.** 10 in. across handles. Mlg. wt. 2¼ lbs.

102 Breakfast Plate Set. $3.75 **with PREMIUM.** THREE 8½ in. Mlg. wt. 3¼ lbs.

103 Butter Tub. $1.70 **with PREMIUM.** Diam., 5⅛ in. Drainer. Mlg. wt. 1¼ lbs.

115 Jug. $2.40 **with PREMIUM.** One qt. size. Height, 5¾ in. Mlg. wt. 1¾ lbs.

116 Egg Cup Set. $1.40 **with PREMIUM.** Four cups, 3⅛ in. high. Mlg. wt. 1¼ lbs.

117 Syrup Jug. $2.10 **with PREM.** Covered jug, 4½ in. high, and plate. Wt. 1¼ lbs.

118 Celery Tray. $2.80 **with PREM.** 12¼ in. long. Mlg. wt. 1¾ lbs.

131 Relish Dish. $1.10 **with PREM.** 7 x 5 in. Mlg. wt. 12 oz.

132 After-Dinner Cup-and-Saucer Set. $3.50 **with PREM.** Six cups, 2⅛ in. high and six 4¼-in. saucers. Mlg. wt. 2½ lbs.

133 Bouillon Cup-and-Saucer Set. $4.80 **with PREM.** Six 3½-in. cups, and saucers for consomme, soups, etc. Mlg. wt. 4 lbs.

134 Salt and Pepper Shakers. 65c **with PREMIUM.** 3 in. high. Mlg wt 6 oz.

173 Small Open Vegetable Dish. $2.25 **with PREMIUM.** 9¼ in. across handles, 6¾ in. wide. Mlg. wt. 1½ lbs.

195 Pickle Set. $1.00 **with PREM.** Handled plate, 5½ in. in diam. 4¾-in. decorated bone fork. Mlg. wt. 10 oz.

196 Berry Sugar and Cream Set. $2 **with PREMIUM.** Sugar shaker, 6½ in. high; pitcher, 5¾ in. high. Mlg. wt. 1¼ lbs.

197 Sugar and Cream Set. $2.00 **with PREMIUM.** Pitcher, 3½ in. high; bowl, 2½ in. Mlg. wt. 1 lb.

198 After-Dinner Coffee Pot. $2 **with PREMIUM.** Capacity, six cups of after-dinner size. Mlg. wt. 1¼ lbs.

199 Mustard Pot. 60c **with PREM.** Jar, 2¾ in. in diameter; 1⅞ in. high. Has notched cover and spoon. Mlg. wt. 8 oz.

200 Individual Salt & Pepper Shakers. $1.00 **with PREMIUM.** Set of 4, 2 salt shakers and 2 pepper shakers, 2 5/16 in. high. Mlg. wt. 6 oz.

330 Deep Bowl. $1.40 **with PREM.** Handy size, 5⅛ in. in diameter. Mlg. wt. 1 lb.

331 Platter. $2.50 **with PREM.** Smaller size, 10¼ x 7½ in. Mlg. wt. 1½ lbs.

332 Butter Chip Set. $1.25 **with PREMIUM.** Six 3¼-in. chips. Mlg. wt. 12 oz.

364 Cream Soup Set. $5.00 **with PREMIUM.** THREE smart new cups for cream soup, grapefruit, baked apples, etc. 5⅛ in. in diameter. Can be used on Tea Plates No. 23. Mlg. wt. 4¼ lbs.

Larkin Catalog #107 Spring/Summer 1932.

IMPORTED NORITAKE CHINA

DECORATED in REAL GOLD

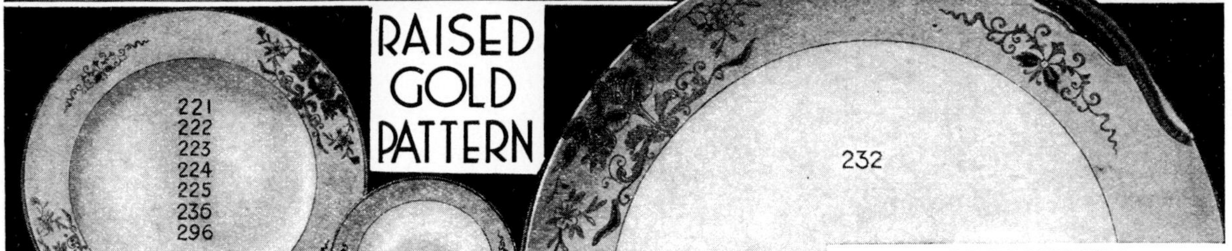

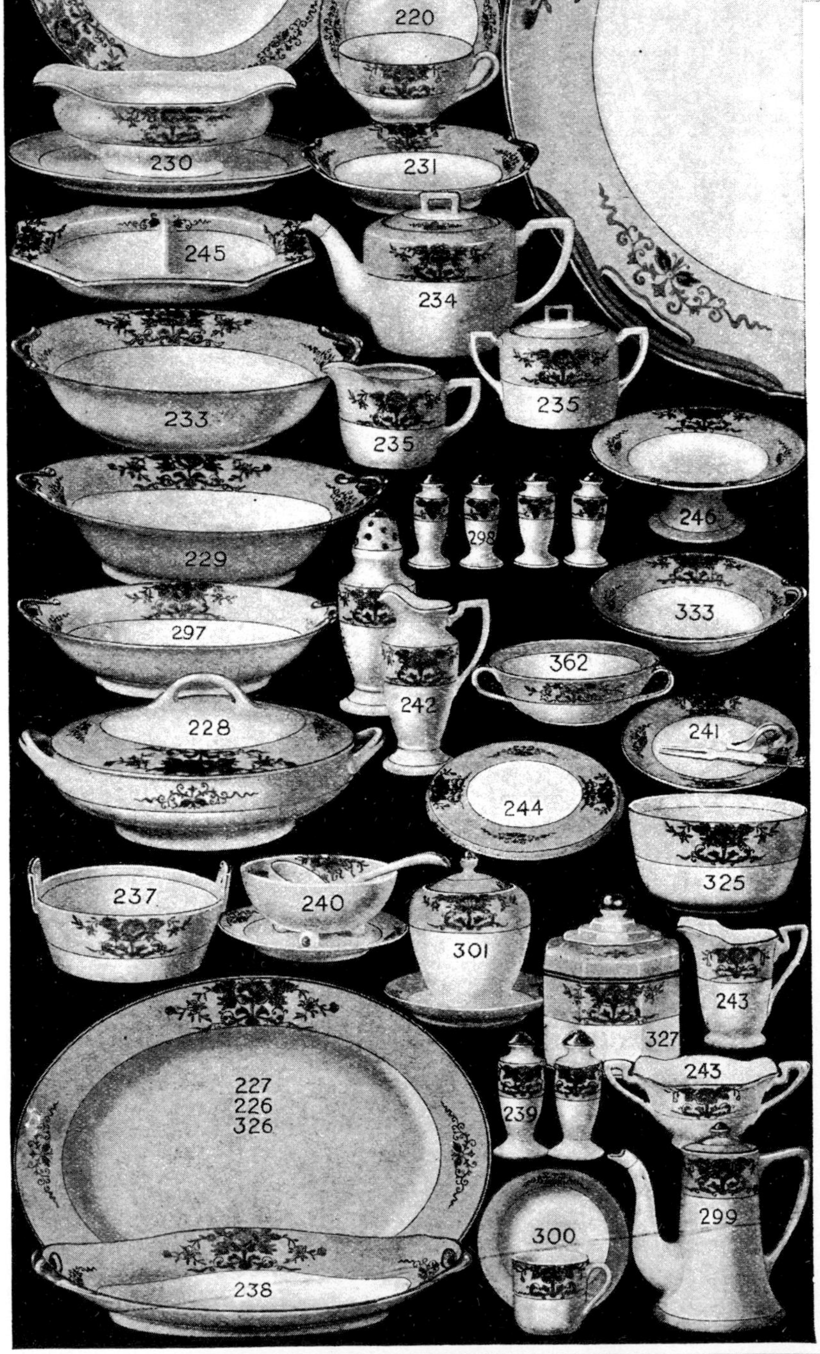

PRICES REDUCED!

Daintily thin yet serviceable. Raised gold medallions on border of ivory with touch of orange and blue in flowers. Gold edges and gold-lined handles attractively enrich the pure white china.

220 Cup-and-Saucer Set. $4.50 **with PREM.** Six Standard size. Mlg. wt. 4 lbs.

221 Bread-and-Butter-Plate Set. $4 **with PREM.** Six 6½-in. plates. Mlg. wt. 3 lbs.

222 Tea Plate Set. $4.50 **with PREM.** Six 7½ in. Wt. 4½ lbs.

223 Dinner Plate Set. $6 **with PREM.** THREE 9¾ in. Mlg. wt. 4½ lbs.

224 Fruit Saucer Set. $3.50 **with PREM.** Six 5¼ in. Mlg. wt. 2¼ lbs.

225 Soup Plate Set. $4 **with PREMIUM.** THREE 7⅛-in. plates. Mlg. wt. 3 lbs.

226 Platter. $4 **with PREM.** 9 x 12 in. Mlg. wt. 2¼ lbs.

227 Platter. $5.20 **with PREM.** 10¼ x 14 in. Mlg. wt. 3¾ lbs.

228 Casserole. $6 **with PREM.** 10¼ in. in diam. Mlg. wt. 3½ lbs.

229 Open Vegetable Dish. $4 **with PREM.** 10½ in. across handles. Mlg. wt. 2 lbs.

230 Gravy Boat. $4 **with PREM.** Width, 5¾ in.; length, 8½ in. Fast stand. Mlg. wt. 1¾ lbs.

231 Handled Relish Dish. $1.50 **with PREM.** 5 x 7 in. Mlg. wt. 12 oz.

232 Cake Plate. $2.50 **with PREM.** Diam., 9¾ in. Mlg. wt. 2 lbs.

233 Salad Bowl. $3 **with PREM.** 10 in. in diam. Mlg. wt. 2¼ lbs.

234 Teapot. $3 **with PREM.** Five-cup size. Height, 4½ in. Mlg. wt. 1¾ lbs.

235 Sugar and Cream Set. $2.50 **with PREM.** Bowl, 3⅝ in. high; pitcher, 3⅛ in. Mlg. wt. 1½ lbs.

236 Oatmeal Dish Set. $4 **with PREM.** Six, 5¾-in. diam. Mlg. wt. 3¼ lbs.

237 Butter Tub. $2.20 **with PREM.** Diam., 5⅛ in. Drainer. Wt. 1¼ lbs.

238 Celery Tray. $3 **with PREM.** 5¾ x 12 in. Mlg. wt. 1¾ lbs.

239 Salt and Pepper Shakers. $1 **with PREM.** Pair, 4 in. high. Mlg. wt. 5 oz.

240 Whipped Cream Set. $2 **with PREM.** 4½-in. bowl, ladle, plate. Mlg. wt. 1 lb.

241 Pickle Set. $1.25 **with PREM.** 5½-in. diam. Bone fork. Mlg. wt. 9 oz.

242 Berry Sugar and Cream Set. $2.50 **with PREM.** Sugar shaker, 6½ in. high; pitcher, 5¾ in. Mlg. wt. 1¼ lbs.

243 Sugar and Cream Set. $2.50 **with PREM.** Pitcher, 3½ in. high; bowl, 2½ in. Mlg. wt. 10 oz.

244 Teapot Tile. $1 **with PREM.** Diam., 6 in. Wt. 12 oz.

245 Relish Dish. $2.50 **with PREM.** 8¼ x 4¾ in. Mlg. wt. 1 lb.

246 Comport. $2.80 **with PREM.** Diam., 6½ in.; 2⅝ in. high. Mlg. wt. 1¼ lbs.

296 Breakfast Plate Set. $4 **with PREM.** THREE 8½ in. Mlg. wt. 3¼ lbs.

297 Vegetable Dish. $3 **with PREMIUM.** 9¼ in. wide. Mlg. wt. 1½ lbs.

298 Individual Salt and Pepper Shakers. $1.10 **with PREM.** Set of four. 2 9/16 in. high. Mlg. wt. 6 oz.

299 After-Dinner Coffee Pot. $2.50 **with PREM.** Holds 6 after-dinner cups. Mlg. wt. 1¼ lbs.

300 After-Dinner Coffee Cup Set. $4.25 **with PREM.** Six cups, 2⅛ in. high; six saucers. Mlg. wt. 2½ lbs.

301 Jam Jar. $2.50 **with PREM.** 5 in. high. 5¼-in. plate; ladle. Mlg. wt. 1½ lbs.

325 Deep Bowl. $1.60 **with PREM.** Diam., 5⅛ in. Mlg. wt. 1 lb.

326 Platter. $3 **with PREM.** 10¼ x 7½ in. The size for cold meats. Mlg. wt. 1½ lbs.

327 Candy Jar. $3 **with PREM.** Diam., 4 in.; 5 in. high. Mlg. wt. 1¼ lbs.

333 Bonbon Dish. $1.25 **with PREM.** Diam., 6¼ in. Mlg. wt. 13 oz.

362 Cream Soup Set. $6 **with PREMIUM.** THREE smart soup cups for use with tea plates. Diam., 5⅛ in. Also for grapefruit or baked apples. Mlg. wt. 4¼ lbs.

Larkin Catalog #109 Spring/Summer 1933.

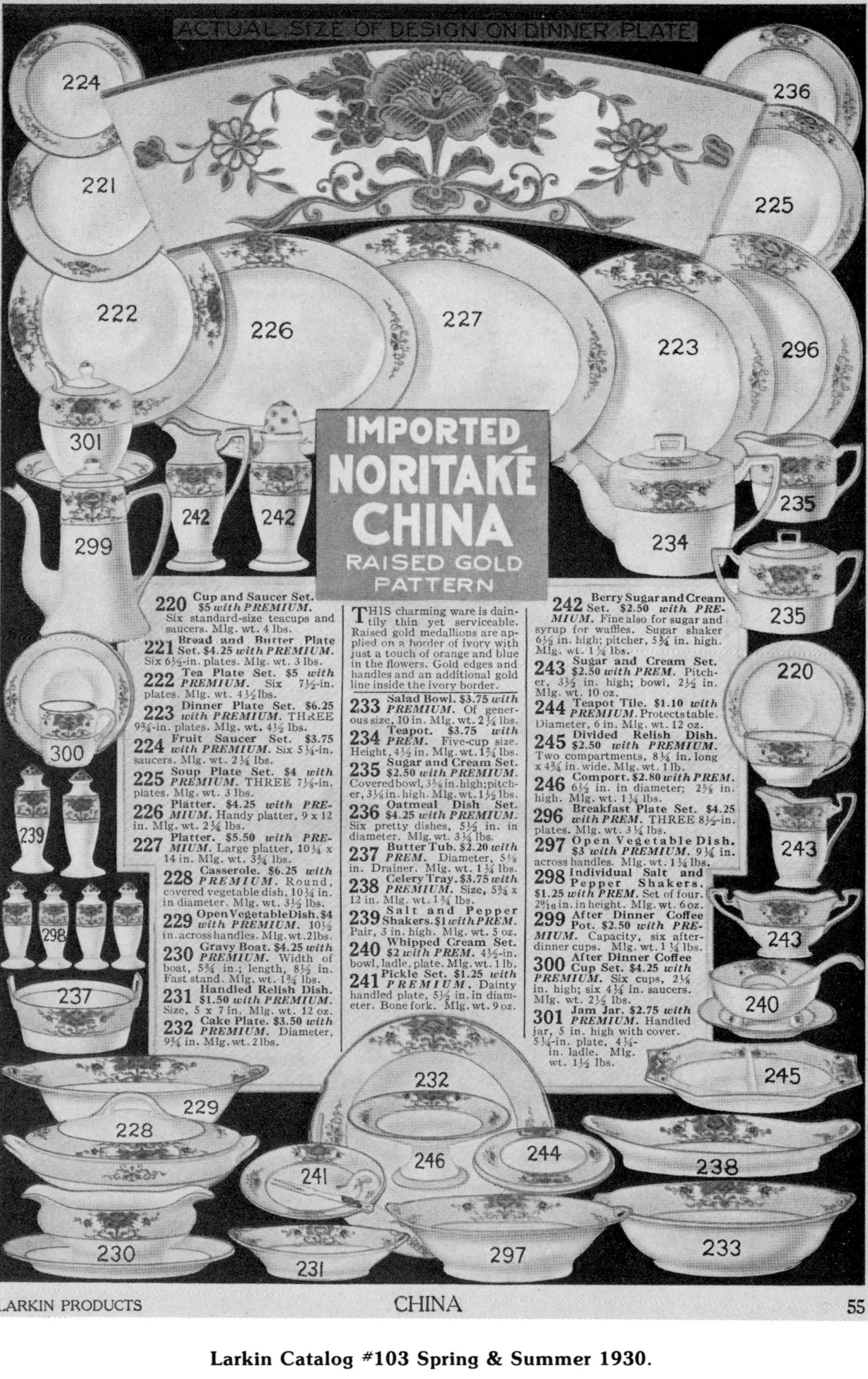

IMPORTED NORITAKÉ CHINA

RAISED GOLD PATTERN

220 Cup and Saucer Set. $5 *with PREMIUM*. Six standard-size teacups and saucers. Mlg. wt. 4 lbs.

221 Bread and Butter Plate Set. $4.25 *with PREMIUM*. Six 6½-in. plates. Mlg. wt. 3 lbs.

222 Tea Plate Set. $5 *with PREMIUM*. Six 7½-in. plates. Mlg. wt. 4½ lbs.

223 Dinner Plate Set. $6.25 *with PREMIUM*. THREE 9¾-in. plates. Mlg. wt. 4½ lbs.

224 Fruit Saucer Set. $3.75 *with PREMIUM*. Six 5¼-in. saucers. Mlg. wt. 2¼ lbs.

225 Soup Plate Set. $4 *with PREMIUM*. THREE 7⅛-in. plates. Mlg. wt. 3 lbs.

226 Platter. $4.25 *with PREMIUM*. Handy platter, 9 x 12 in. Mlg. wt. 2¼ lbs.

227 Platter. $5.50 *with PREMIUM*. Large platter, 10¼ x 14 in. Mlg. wt. 3¾ lbs.

228 Casserole. $6.25 *with PREMIUM*. Round, covered vegetable dish, 10¼ in. in diameter. Mlg. wt. 3½ lbs.

229 Open Vegetable Dish. $4 *with PREMIUM*. 10½ in. across handles. Mlg. wt. 2 lbs.

230 Gravy Boat. $4.25 *with PREMIUM*. Width of boat, 5¾ in.; length, 8½ in. Fast stand. Mlg. wt. 1¾ lbs.

231 Handled Relish Dish. $1.50 *with PREMIUM*. Size, 5 x 7 in. Mlg. wt. 12 oz.

232 Cake Plate. $3.50 *with PREMIUM*. Diameter, 9¾ in. Mlg. wt. 2 lbs.

THIS charming ware is daintily thin yet serviceable. Raised gold medallions are applied on a border of ivory with just a touch of orange and blue in the flowers. Gold edges and handles and an additional gold line inside the ivory border.

233 Salad Bowl. $3.75 *with PREMIUM*. Of generous size, 10 in. Mlg. wt. 2¼ lbs.

234 Teapot. $3.75 *with PREM*. Five-cup size. Height, 4½ in. Mlg. wt. 1¾ lbs.

235 Sugar and Cream Set. $2.50 *with PREMIUM*. Covered bowl, 3⅝ in. high; pitcher, 3⅛ in. high. Mlg. wt. 1½ lbs.

236 Oatmeal Dish Set. $4.25 *with PREMIUM*. Six pretty dishes, 5½ in. in diameter. Mlg. wt. 3¼ lbs.

237 Butter Tub. $2.20 *with PREM*. Diameter, 5⅛ in. Drainer. Mlg. wt. 1¼ lbs.

238 Celery Tray. $3.75 *with PREMIUM*. Size, 5¾ x 12 in. Mlg. wt. 1¾ lbs.

239 Salt and Pepper Shakers. $1 *with PREM*. Pair, 3 in. high. Mlg. wt. 5 oz.

240 Whipped Cream Set. $2 *with PREM*. 4½-in. bowl, ladle, plate. Mlg. wt. 1 lb.

241 Pickle Set. $1.25 *with PREMIUM*. Dainty handled plate, 5½ in. in diameter. Bone fork. Mlg. wt. 9 oz.

242 Berry Sugar and Cream Set. $2.50 *with PREMIUM*. Fine also for sugar and syrup for waffles. Sugar shaker 6½ in. high; pitcher, 5¾ in. high. Mlg. wt. 1¼ lbs.

243 Sugar and Cream Set. $2.50 *with PREM*. Pitcher, 3½ in. high; bowl, 2½ in. Mlg. wt. 10 oz.

244 Teapot Tile. $1.10 *with PREMIUM*. Protects table. Diameter, 6 in. Mlg. wt. 12 oz.

245 Divided Relish Dish. $2.50 *with PREMIUM*. Two compartments, 8¼ in. long x 4¾ in. wide. Mlg. wt. 1 lb.

246 Comport. $2.80 *with PREM*. 6½ in. in diameter; 2⅝ in. high. Mlg. wt. 1¼ lbs.

296 Breakfast Plate Set. $4.25 *with PREM*. THREE 8½-in. plates. Mlg. wt. 3¼ lbs.

297 Open Vegetable Dish. $3 *with PREMIUM*. 9¼ in. across handles. Mlg. wt. 1¼ lbs.

298 Individual Salt and Pepper Shakers. $1.25 *with PREM*. Set of four. 2 9/16 in. in height. Mlg. wt. 6 oz.

299 After Dinner Coffee Pot. $2.50 *with PREMIUM*. Capacity, six after-dinner cups. Mlg. wt. 1¼ lbs.

300 After Dinner Coffee Cup Set. $4.25 *with PREMIUM*. Six cups, 2⅛ in. high; six 4¼ in. saucers. Mlg. wt. 2½ lbs.

301 Jam Jar. $2.75 *with PREMIUM*. Handled jar, 5 in. high with cover. 5¼-in. plate, 4¼-in. ladle. Mlg. wt. 1½ lbs.

LARKIN PRODUCTS CHINA 55

Larkin Catalog #103 Spring & Summer 1930.

NORITAKE'

China Dinnerware

RAISED GOLD PATTERN

DECORATED IN REAL GOLD

PATTERN EXCLUSIVE WITH LARKIN CO

OPEN STOCK

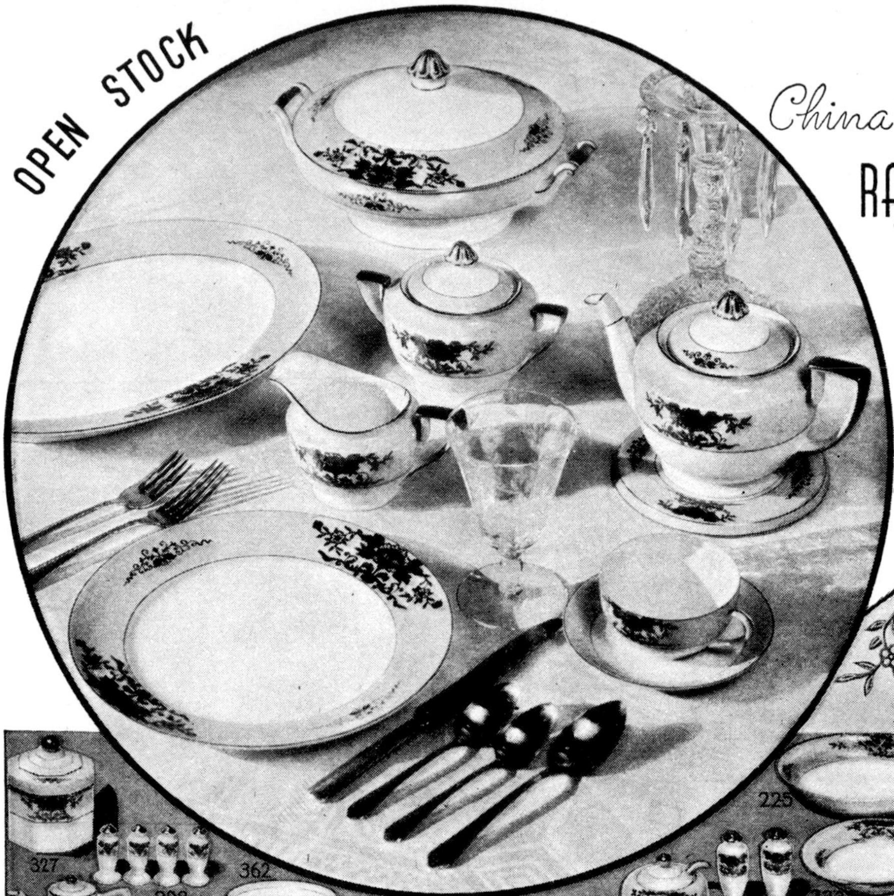

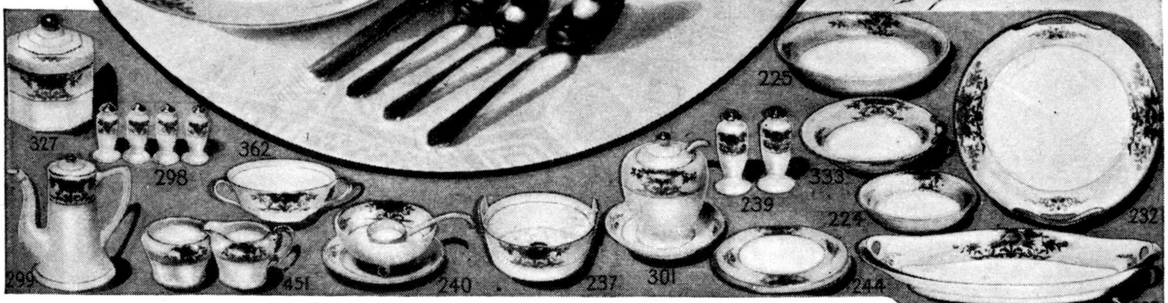

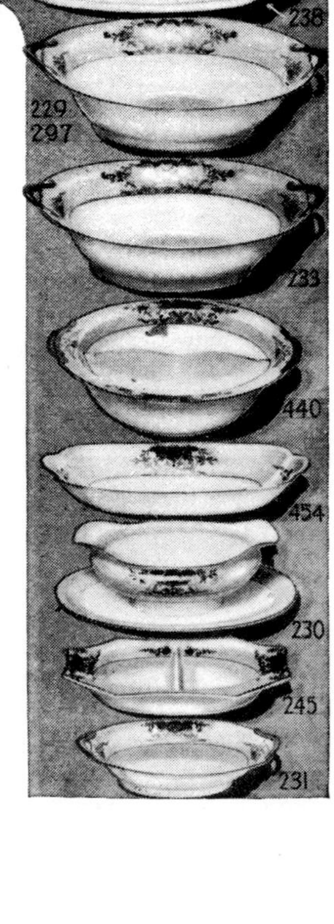

Wonderfully rich in appearance and daintily thin, yet serviceable, this lovely Raised Gold pattern is a great favorite with a host of Larkin customers. The artistic raised medallions are decorated in ***real gold*** on a border of ivory with just a touch of orange and blue in the flowers.

The body is pure white with gold edges and an additional gold line inside border and gold edges giving added richness and smart contrast. The varied selection enables you to assemble the set you want or add to it from time to time.

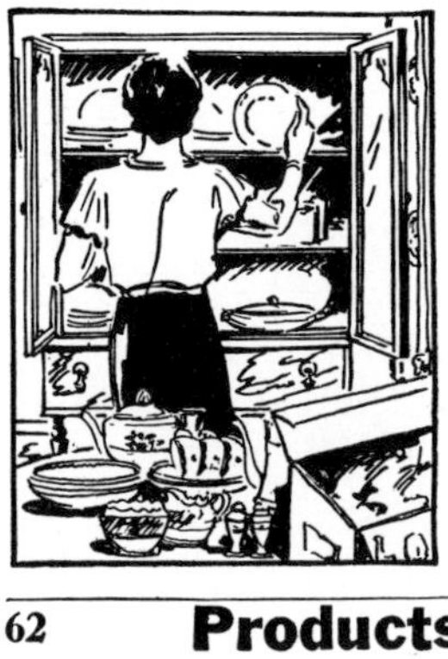

Item	No	*With Prem.*	*Cash Price*	Size	Mlg. Wt.
Cup-and-Saucer Set (6)	**220**	**$4.70**	**$2.35**	Standard	4 lbs.
Bread-and-Butter Plate Set (6)	**221**	**4.00**	**2.00**	6½ in.	3 lbs.
Tea Plate Set (6)	**222**	**4.70**	**2.35**	7½ in.	4½ lbs.
Dinner Plate Set (3)	**223**	**6.00**	**3.00**	9¾ in.	4¼ lbs.
Fruit Saucer Set (6)	**224**	**3.50**	**1.75**	5¼ in.	2¼ lbs.
Soup Plate Set (3)	**225**	**4.00**	**2.00**	7⅛ in.	3 lbs.
Platter	**226**	**4.30**	**2.15**	9 x 12 in.	2¼ lbs.
Platter	**227**	**5.50**	**2.75**	10½ x 14 in.	3½ lbs.
Open Vegetable Dish	**229**	**4.00**	**2.00**	10½ in. long	2 lbs.
Gravy Boat	**230**	**4.00**	**2.00**	8½ in. long	1¾ lbs.
Handled Relish Dish	**231**	**1.50**	**.75**	5 x 7 in.	12 oz.
Cake Plate	**232**	**2.50**	**1.25**	9¾ in.	2 lbs.
Salad Bowl	**233**	**3.00**	**1.50**	10 in.	2¼ lbs.
Oatmeal Dish Set (6)	**236**	**3.80**	**1.90**	5¾ in.	3¼ lbs.
Butter Tub	**237**	**2.00**	**1.00**	5⅛ in.	1¼ lbs.
Celery Tray	**238**	**3.20**	**1.60**	5¾ x 12 in.	1¾ lbs.
Salt and Pepper Shakers (Pair)	**239**	**1.00**	**.50**	4 in. high	5 oz.
Whipped Cream or Mayonnaise Set	**240**	**2.20**	**1.10**	4½ in. bowl	1 lb.
Teapot Tile	**244**	**1.00**	**.50**	6 in.	12 oz.
Relish Dish	**245**	**2.50**	**1.25**	4¾ x 8¼ in.	1 lb.
Breakfast Plate Set (3)	**296**	**4.50**	**2.25**	8½ in.	3¼ lbs.
Vegetable Dish	**297**	**3.00**	**1.50**	9¼ in.	1½ lbs.
Indiv. Salt & Pepper Shakers (4)	**298**	**1.00**	**.50**	2³⁄₁₆ in.	6 oz.
After-Dinner Coffee Pot	**299**	**2.50**	**1.25**	6 A.D. cups	1¼ lbs.
Jam Jar	**301**	**2.50**	**1.25**	5 in. high	1½ lbs.
Candy or Tobacco Jar	**327**	**3.00**	**1.50**	5 in. high	1¼ lbs.
Bonbon Dish	**333**	**1.20**	**.60**	6¼ in.	13 oz.
Cream Soup Set (3)	**362**	**6.00**	**3.00**	5⅛ in.	1½ lbs.
Casserole	**402**	**6.00**	**3.00**	10¼ in.	3 lbs.
Sugar and Cream Set	**437**	**2.60**	**1.30**	Bowl, 3⅝ in. high	1½ lbs.
Divided Vegetable Dish	**440**	**4.50**	**2.25**	9½ in.	2 lbs.
Teapot	**443**	**3.00**	**1.50**	4½ in. high	1¾ lbs.
Sugar and Cream Set	**451**	**2.00**	**1.00**	2¼ in. high	12 oz.
Celery Tray	**454**	**1.60**	**.80**	4⅜ x 10 in.	1 lb.

62 **Products**

Larkin Catalog #121 Spring/Summer 1939.

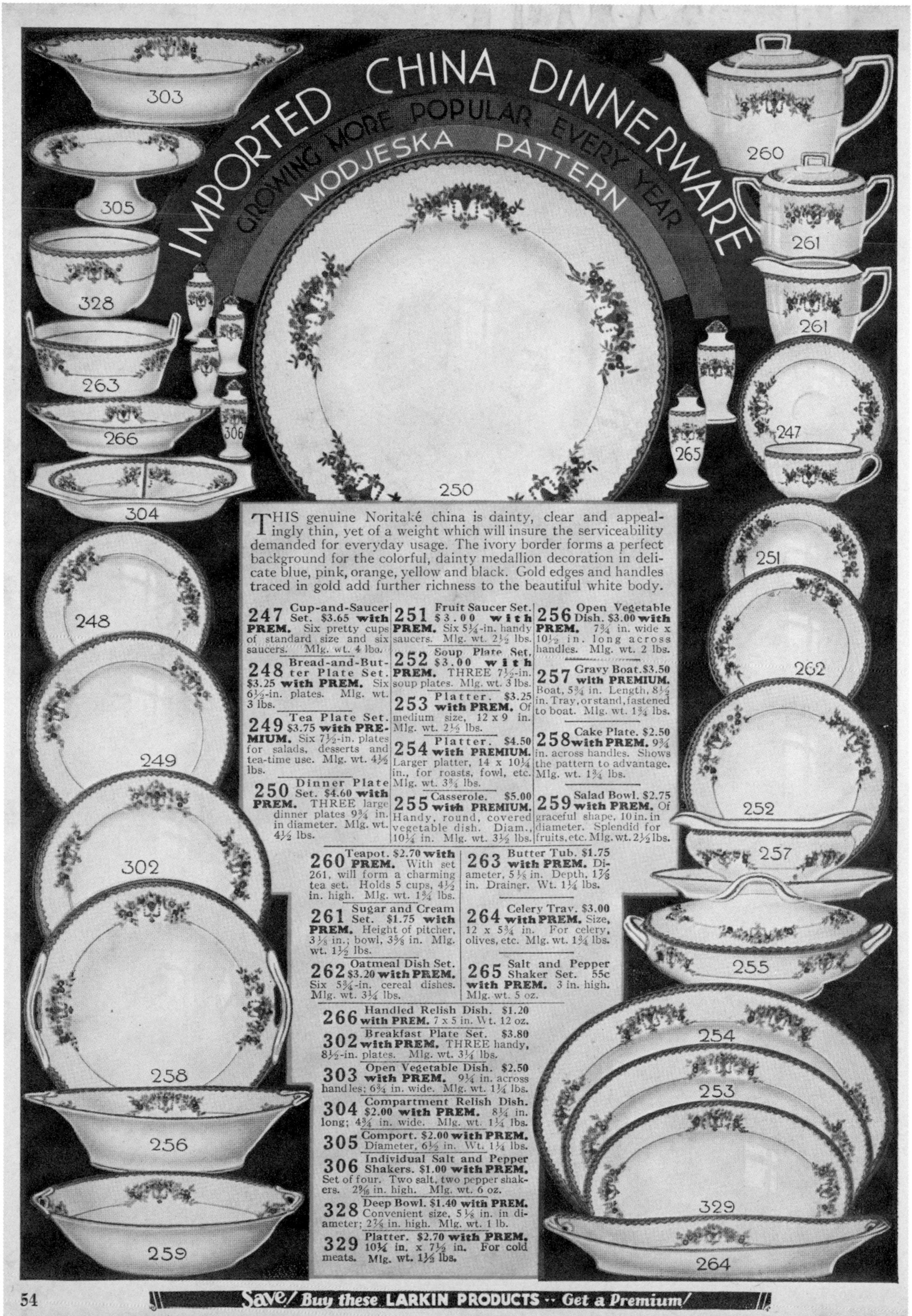
IMPORTED CHINA DINNERWARE
GROWING MORE POPULAR EVERY YEAR
MODJESKA PATTERN
303
305
328
263
266
306
304
260
261
261
247
265
250
THIS genuine Noritaké china is dainty, clear and appealingly thin, yet of a weight which will insure the serviceability demanded for everyday usage. The ivory border forms a perfect background for the colorful, dainty medallion decoration in delicate blue, pink, orange, yellow and black. Gold edges and handles traced in gold add further richness to the beautiful white body.
247 Cup-and-Saucer Set. $3.65 with PREM. Six pretty cups of standard size and six saucers. Mlg. wt. 4 lbs.
248 Bread-and-Butter Plate Set. $3.25 with PREM. Six 6½-in. plates. Mlg. wt. 3 lbs.
249 Tea Plate Set. $3.75 with PREMIUM. Six 7½-in. plates for salads, desserts and tea-time use. Mlg. wt. 4½ lbs.
250 Dinner Plate Set. $4.60 with PREM. THREE large dinner plates 9¾ in. in diameter. Mlg. wt. 4½ lbs.
251 Fruit Saucer Set. $3.00 with PREM. Six 5¼-in. handy saucers. Mlg. wt. 2½ lbs.
252 Soup Plate Set. $3.00 with PREM. THREE 7½-in. soup plates. Mlg. wt. 3 lbs.
253 Platter. $3.25 with PREM. Of medium size, 12 x 9 in. Mlg. wt. 2½ lbs.
254 Platter. $4.50 with PREMIUM. Larger platter, 14 x 10¼ in., for roasts, fowl, etc. Mlg. wt. 3¾ lbs.
255 Casserole. $5.00 with PREMIUM. Handy, round, covered vegetable dish. Diam., 10¼ in. Mlg. wt. 3½ lbs.
256 Open Vegetable Dish. $3.00 with PREM. 7¾ in. wide x 10½ in. long across handles. Mlg. wt. 2 lbs.
257 Gravy Boat. $3.50 with PREMIUM. Boat, 5¾ in. Length, 8½ in. Tray, or stand, fastened to boat. Mlg. wt. 1¾ lbs.
258 Cake Plate. $2.50 with PREM. 9¾ in. across handles. Shows the pattern to advantage. Mlg. wt. 1¾ lbs.
259 Salad Bowl. $2.75 with PREM. Of graceful shape, 10 in. in diameter. Splendid for fruits, etc. Mlg. wt. 2½ lbs.
260 Teapot. $2.70 with PREM. With set 261, will form a charming tea set. Holds 5 cups, 4½ in. high. Mlg. wt. 1¾ lbs.
261 Sugar and Cream Set. $1.75 with PREM. Height of pitcher, 3⅛ in.; bowl, 3⅝ in. Mlg. wt. 1½ lbs.
262 Oatmeal Dish Set. $3.20 with PREM. Six 5¾-in. cereal dishes. Mlg. wt. 3¼ lbs.
263 Butter Tub. $1.75 with PREM. Diameter, 5⅛ in. Depth, 1⅞ in. Drainer. Wt. 1¼ lbs.
264 Celery Tray. $3.00 with PREM. Size, 12 x 5¾ in. For celery, olives, etc. Mlg. wt. 1¾ lbs.
265 Salt and Pepper Shaker Set. 55c with PREM. 3 in. high. Mlg. wt. 5 oz.
266 Handled Relish Dish. $1.20 with PREM. 7 x 5 in. Wt. 12 oz.
302 Breakfast Plate Set. $3.80 with PREM. THREE handy, 8½-in. plates. Mlg. wt. 3¼ lbs.
303 Open Vegetable Dish. $2.50 with PREM. 9¼ in. across handles; 6¾ in. wide. Mlg. wt. 1¼ lbs.
304 Compartment Relish Dish. $2.00 with PREM. 8¼ in. long; 4¾ in. wide. Mlg. wt. 1¼ lbs.
305 Comport. $2.00 with PREM. Diameter, 6½ in. Wt. 1¼ lbs.
306 Individual Salt and Pepper Shakers. $1.00 with PREM. Set of four. Two salt, two pepper shakers. 2 9/16 in. high. Mlg. wt. 6 oz.
328 Deep Bowl. $1.40 with PREM. Convenient size, 5⅛ in. in diameter; 2⅞ in. high. Mlg. wt. 1 lb.
329 Platter. $2.70 with PREM. 10¼ in. x 7½ in. For cold meats. Mlg. wt. 1⅓ lbs.
248
249
302
258
256
259
251
262
252
257
255
254
253
329
264
54
Save! Buy these LARKIN PRODUCTS -- Get a Premium!

Larking Catalog #108 Fall/Winter 1932.

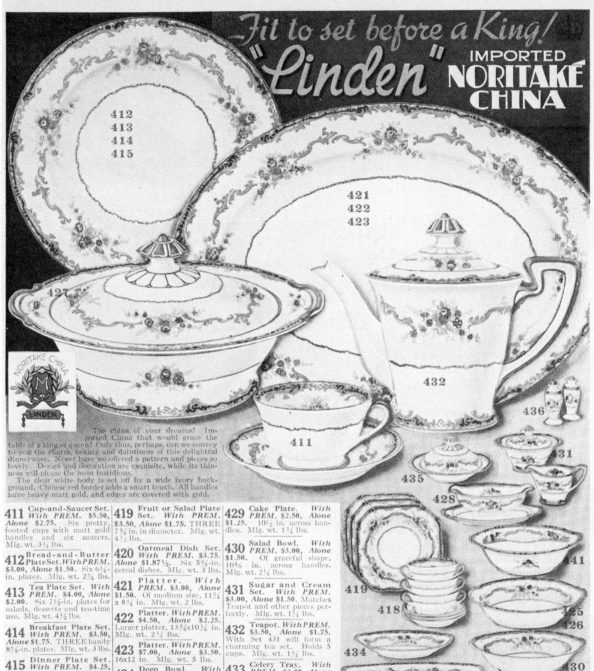

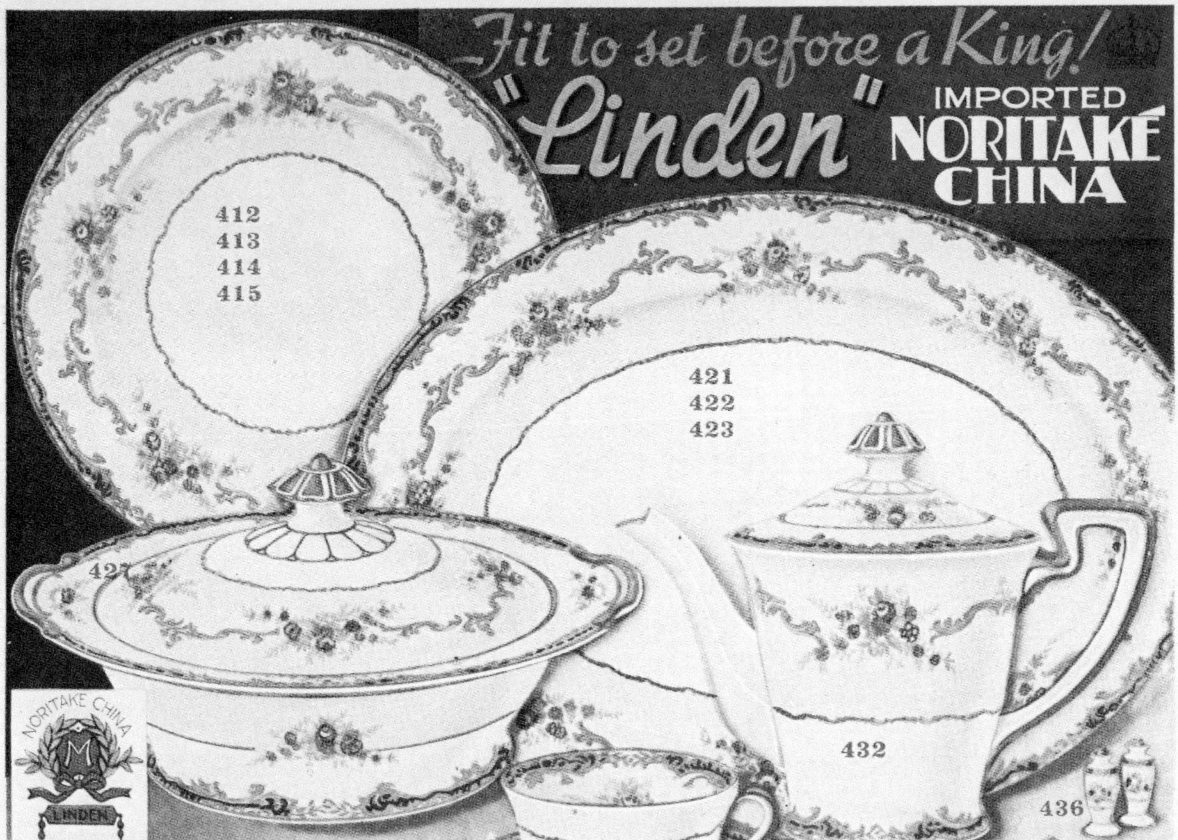
Fit to set before a King!
"Linden" IMPORTED NORITAKÉ CHINA
412
413
414
415
421
422
423
432
436
NORITAKE CHINA
LINDEN

The china of your dreams! Imported China that would grace the table of a king or queen! Only thus, perhaps, can we convey to you the charm, beauty and daintiness of this delightful dinnerware. Never have we offered a pattern and pieces so lovely. Design and decoration are exquisite, while its thinness will please the most fastidious.

The clear white body is set off by a wide ivory background. Chinese red border adds a smart touch. All handles have heavy matt gold, and edges are covered with gold.

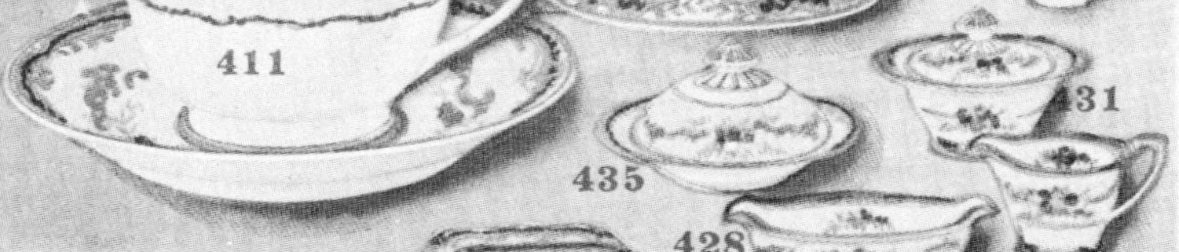
411
435
428

411 Cup-and-Saucer Set. *With PREM.* $5.50, *Alone* $2.75. Six pretty, footed cups with matt gold handles and six saucers. Mlg. wt. $3\frac{3}{4}$ lbs.

412 Bread-and-Butter Plate Set. *With PREM.* $3.00, *Alone* $1.50. Six $6\frac{1}{4}$-in. plates. Mlg. wt. $2\frac{3}{4}$ lbs.

413 Tea Plate Set. *With PREM.* $4.00, *Alone* $2.00. Six $7\frac{1}{2}$-in. plates for salads, desserts and tea-time use. Mlg. wt. $4\frac{1}{2}$ lbs.

414 Breakfast Plate Set. *With PREM.* $3.50, *Alone* $1.75. THREE handy $8\frac{5}{8}$-in. plates. Mlg. wt. 3 lbs.

415 Dinner Plate Set. *With PREM.* $4.25, *Alone* $2.12½. THREE large dinner plates $9\frac{3}{4}$ in. in diameter. Mlg. wt. $4\frac{1}{4}$ lbs.

416 Fruit Saucer Set. *With PREM.* $3.00, *Alone* $1.50. Six $5\frac{1}{4}$-in., handy saucers. Mlg. wt. $2\frac{1}{2}$ lbs.

417 Soup Plate Set. *With PREM.* $3.25, *Alone* $1.62½. THREE $7\frac{3}{8}$-in. plates. Mlg. wt. $2\frac{3}{4}$ lbs.

418 Cream Soup Set. *With PREM.* $5.75, *Alone* $2.87½. THREE smart cups for cream soup, grapefruit, baked apples, etc., $4\frac{1}{2}$ in. in diameter, and THREE $7\frac{1}{8}$-in. plates to go with them. These plates are fine, too, for desserts and a host of other uses. Mlg. wt. $1\frac{1}{2}$ lbs.

419 Fruit or Salad Plate Set. *With PREM.* $3.50, *Alone* $1.75. THREE $7\frac{3}{4}$ in. in diameter. Mlg. wt. $4\frac{1}{2}$ lbs.

420 Oatmeal Dish Set. *With PREM.* $3.75. *Alone* $1.87½. Six $5\frac{3}{4}$-in. cereal dishes. Mlg. wt. 3 lbs.

421 Platter. *With PREM.* $3.00, *Alone* $1.50. Of medium size, $11\frac{3}{4}$ x $8\frac{3}{4}$ in. Mlg. wt. 2 lbs.

422 Platter. *With PREM.* $4.50, *Alone* $2.25. Larger platter, $13\frac{3}{4}$x$10\frac{1}{4}$ in. Mlg. wt. $2\frac{1}{4}$ lbs.

423 Platter. *With PREM.* $7.00, *Alone* $3.50. 16x12 in. Mlg. wt. 5 lbs.

424 Deep Bowl. *With PREM.* $1.40, *Alone* 70c. $5\frac{1}{8}$ in. in diameter; $2\frac{7}{8}$ in. high. Mlg. wt. 14 oz.

425 Open Vegetable Dish. *With PREM.* $2.75, *Alone* $1.37½. $10\frac{1}{2}$ in. across handles; $7\frac{5}{8}$ in. wide. Mlg. wt. $1\frac{3}{4}$ lbs.

426 Open Vegetable Dish. *With PREM.* $2.25, *Alone* $1.12½. 9 in. across handles, by $6\frac{1}{2}$ in. wide. Mlg. wt. $1\frac{1}{2}$ lbs.

427 Casserole. *With PREM.* $5.50, *Alone* $2.75. Handy, round, covered vegetable dish. Diameter $10\frac{1}{4}$ in. Mlg. wt. $3\frac{1}{4}$ lbs.

428 Gravy Boat. *With PREM.* $3.50, *Alone* $1.75. Boat, $7\frac{1}{2}$ in. Length, 9 in. Tray, or stand, fastened to boat. Mlg. wt. $1\frac{3}{4}$ lbs.

429 Cake Plate. *With PREM.* $2.50, *Alone* $1.25. $10\frac{1}{2}$ in. across handles. Mlg. wt. $1\frac{3}{4}$ lbs.

430 Salad Bowl. *With PREM.* $3.00, *Alone* $1.50. Of graceful shape, $10\frac{3}{8}$ in. across handles. Mlg. wt. $2\frac{1}{4}$ lbs.

431 Sugar and Cream Set. *With PREM.* $3.00, *Alone* $1.50. Matches Teapot and other pieces perfectly. Mlg. wt. $1\frac{1}{4}$ lbs.

432 Teapot. *With PREM.* $3.50, *Alone* $1.75. With Set 431 will form a charming tea set. Holds 5 cups. Mlg. wt. $1\frac{3}{4}$ lbs.

433 Celery Tray. *With PREM.* $3.00, *Alone* $1.50. Size, $12\frac{7}{8}$x$6\frac{1}{4}$ in. Mlg. wt. $1\frac{1}{2}$ lbs.

434 Pickle Dish. *With PREM.* $1.50, *Alone* 75c. Measures $8\frac{5}{8}$ in. Mlg. wt. 12 oz.

435 Butter Dish. *With PREM.* $2.75, *Alone* $1.37½. Plate, $7\frac{3}{8}$ in. in diameter, with attractive gold-trimmed knob on cover. Mlg. wt. $1\frac{1}{2}$ lbs.

436 Salt and Pepper Shaker Set. *Pair with PREM.* 70c, *Alone* 35c. 4 in. high. Mlg. wt. 7 oz.

441 *Divided Vegetable Dish. With PREM.* $3.50, *Alone* $1.75. Diam. $9\frac{1}{2}$ in. Serves two vegetables separated by partition in center. Mlg. wt. 2 lbs.

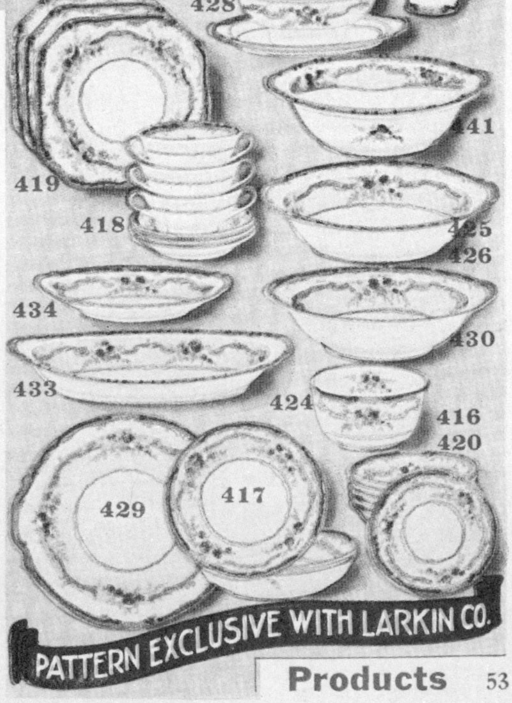
419
418
441
434
430
433
424
416
420
429
417
PATTERN EXCLUSIVE WITH LARKIN CO.

Products 53

Larkin Catalog #115 Spring/Summer 1936.

Composition of all "Noritake" Dinner-Sets

This imported "Noritake" China comes to us direct from abroad. By the Larkin Plan it is yours on terms that actually give you a two-dollar value for one. It is beautifully clear and white—fine and dainty enough to please the most fastidious. Delicately decorated in charming designs retouched by hand.

Briarcliff Dinner-Sets

Set	No.	Given with Products	Shpg. Wt.
50-piece	4538	$54.00	60 lbs.
66-piece	4541	68.00	72 lbs.
95-piece	4536	100.00	103 lbs.

Charming border-design of dark-blue and black interspersed with wreaths of hand-painted pink roses and green leaves. A wide band of old ivory edged with black, enhances the beauty of this set.

Bright gold edges and coin-gold handles.

Savoy Dinner-Sets

Set	No.	Given with Products	Shpg. Wt.
50-piece	4533	$60.00	60 lbs.
66-piece	4532	76.00	72 lbs.
95-piece	4531	110.00	103 lbs.

Has wide ivory border striped with light-brown lines. Hand-painted medallions of pink roses with green leaves. Pattern is embellished with a narrow blue and black conventional design around outer edge. Bright gold edges and coin-gold handles.

All 95-piece Sets:
12 Bread-and-Butter-Plates
12 Tea-Plates
12 Dinner-Plates
12 Soup-Plates
12 Fruit-Saucers
12 Tea-Cups and Saucers
1 Pickle-Dish
1 Small Platter
1 Large Platter
1 Casserole (2 pieces)
1 Open Vegetable-Dish
1 Gravy-Boat (fast stand)
1 Sugar-Bowl (2 pieces)
1 Cream-Pitcher
1 Salad-Bowl

All 66-piece Sets:
8 Bread-and-Butter-Plates
8 Tea-Plates
8 Dinner-Plates
8 Soup-Plates
8 Fruit-Saucers
8 Tea-Cups and Saucers
1 Small Platter
1 Medium Platter
1 Casserole (2 pieces)
1 Open Vegetable-Dish
1 Gravy-Boat (with fast stand)
1 Pickle-Dish
1 Sugar-Bowl (2 pieces)
1 Cream-Pitcher

All 50-piece Sets:
6 Bread-and-Butter-Plates
6 Tea-Plates
6 Dinner-Plates
6 Soup-Plates
6 Fruit-Saucers
6 Tea-Cups and Saucers
1 Small Platter
1 Casserole (2 pieces)
1 Open Vegetable-Dish
1 Gravy-Boat (with fast stand)
1 Sugar-Bowl (2 pieces)
1 Cream-Pitcher

Sizes of Plates: Dinner-Plates, 9⅞ in.; Bread-and-Butter-Plates, 6½ in.; Tea-Plates, 7¼ in.; Soup-Plates, 7⅜ in.; Small Platters, 11¾ in.; Medium Platters, 14 in.; Large Platters, 16 in.

Sample Bread-and-Butter-Plate of Noritake Sets postpaid 25c cash.

LARKIN DINNER-SETS MAY BE BOUGHT FOR CASH AT ONE-HALF COUPON PRICE.   SEE PAGE 4.

Larkin Catalog #90 Fall/Winter 1923-24.

Linden #413 tea plate.

Briarcliff tea plate.

Azalea #2 cup and saucers; #7 sugar & cream set.

Sheridan #34 cake plate.

Tree in the Meadow #318; candy jar.

Raised Gold #333 bon bon dish; #242 berry sugar & cream set.

Modjeska #249 tea plate.

Raised Gold #243 sugar & cream set.

Designs and Techniques Used on Noritake Wares

Close-up of handpainting.

Close-up of decal.

Being a "Nipponologist" I had already researched pieces produced in the Nippon time period (1891-1921). When I began collecting the later Noritake pieces I was naturally interested in noting the differences that I found between these years of production. I noticed a conspicuous absence of wares decorated in moriage fashion, also those employing the tapestry technique, the use of beading and incised decoration. Some of these are not found in great abundance on the Nippon pieces but do crop up from time to time. However, I was hard pressed to find any pieces made during the 1921-41 period employing these techniques. I do believe a few must exist but so far they have not been brought to my attention. If they do exist it is most likely that they were manufactured in the early twenties following the trend set during the Nippon years. It does make one wonder why they "disappeared" as they had been so popular. Most of these techinques did require a great deal more work than the others and perhaps in an effort to keep the prices as low as possible they were discontinued in favor of the use of decals or perhaps it was just a sign of the times and they lost favor with the general public. Decals gave the appearance of hand painting but could be applied quickly and inexpensively.

Decals or decalcomanias often appear to be hand painting to the untrained eye. The color stayed within the lines whereas pieces decorated with transfer prints seemed to have the color running out of the lines. Both types of decoration were often touched up by hand painting. Decals permit the use of a number of colors simultaneously and are generally of a complex nature, for example the portraits we find on pieces would have been virtually impossible to duplicate time and time again and would also have been prohibitive in cost. Decals and transfer prints are an inexpensive substitute for hand painted decoration. This style of decorating is often difficult to detect, however, if one looks under a high power magnifying glass the print appears to have tiny dots making up the design. On some items decals were used for the majority of the design with the artist outlining only with a little trim. Often, the center of a plate or bowl will have transfer work but the border will be hand painted or vice versa. When used in conjunction with hand painting the item could then truthfully bear the backstamp of hand painted Noritake as some of it actually had been hand painted. Both the decal and the hand painted touches could be fired at the same time making this a very economical way to produce the wares.

When items have sprigged-on decoration it merely means that two or more pieces were used and joined together. Sprigging is the application of small molded relief decoration to the surface of the item as in Wedgwood's Jasper ware. This type of decoration is made separately in sprig molds.

A sprig mold is a one piece mold which is used in making sprigging ornaments or any type of item where only one side of the piece is molded. The decoration is incised into the mold. Moist clay is rolled out and squeezed into the mold until every bit of the plaster mold is filled. The excess clay is scraped off with a modeling tool. After the item has dried it is carefully lifted out. The finished item will be the exact reverse of the mold, whatever is incised into the mold will protrude out on the porcelain piece. Only one side is molded and the exposed side becomes the back of the finished item. Liquid or casting slip may also be poured into sprig molds in place of the plastic clay. When used as a sprigging ornament, both figures and vessels must be dampened with water or liquid clay to make them adhere. Only slight pressure is needed as too much might spoil the detail of the ornament.

On Jasper ware items the relief decoration can be found in the shapes of cameos, portraits, raised figures, ornamental scrolls and designs and medallions. Jasper ware items are generally found in light blue and sage green colors and are decorated with white sprigged-on-bas-reliefs. Blue Jasper ware was achieved by the addition of cobalt to the clay and the green color was made by adding both cobalt and iron. The Japanese attempted to copy this classical style of pottery using the established blue and green Jasper ware background colors. However, on these items we find that slip trailing is often used for the decoration rather than the sprigging technique employed on Jasper ware.

Silhouettes are another popular form of decoration during this time period. These profile drawings and portraits usually have the outline filled in with black while a few employ other colors in their decoration. We often find elegant ladies with bouffant dresses and pompadour hair styles or cloche hats. There are gentlemen dressed in top hats and capes in the elegant manner of the time period.

The Art Nouveau style pieces had pretty well faded out by the twenties but a few Noritake pieces can still be found. The word Art Nouveau is derived from the French words meaning new art. During the period of 1885-1925 artists tended to use bolder colors and realism was rejected. Free flowing designs were used breaking away from the imitations of the past. It was a period of "new style". Commonly found patterns have tendril-like forms, sweeping and flowing lines, elongated figures and flowers and leaves. Many of the Art Nouveau maidens were portrayed with long flowing hair. Although historians do date this style lasting as long as 1925, its popularity waned after 1910.

Etched gold means engraving by "biting out by acid" on the pieces whereas gold overlay or raised gold is gold built up on the item. Many of these wares will be found on a cobalt background. The gold was fired separately after all the other decorating was done as gold melts at a much lower temperature. Otherwise it would melt into the other decor. If slightly overfired the gold becomes discolored so pieces decorated in this manner had to be treated very carefully.

The Art Deco look is found on many of the Noritake items. It is a "modernist" style employing bright colors, geometric shapes and highly stylized designs and characteristics. In 1925 the Exposition des Arts Decoratifs et Industriels Modernes was held in Paris. This defined and celebrated this new style and the name Art Deco is an anglicized abbreviation derived in 1960 when interest in the style was revived. It is also known as Art Moderne and Modernistic. Art Deco emerged as a reaction to Art Nouveau and proved to be the antithesis to it. It pervaded the arts through the 20's and 30's until World War II.

Commedia dell'arte was very popular in Italy from the mid sixteenth to the mid eighteenth century. A modern revival of this improvised Italian comedy began in the twentieth century and some of the characters are found decorating the Noritake wares.

Commedia dell'arte was originally performed by wandering troupes of professional actors who performed using mimic expressions or pantomime. Many of the actors wore masks which covered the upper half of their face. Each was unique, some had pointed noses, others round, some had slit eyes, others oval. Commedia dell'arte is also known as "the comedy of masks".

The four main characters featured were Harlequin, Columbine, Pierrot and Punchinello. Harlequin was a stock character in this comic theater. He frolics and acts like a clown. He is witty, athletic and shrewd but a fool in the matters of love. He plays the role of the agile, mischievous, amorous servant or so-called zanni. Harlequin wears a tight fitting costume covered with diamond-shaped patches of bright colors. Mauve stands for fidelity, black means invisibility, scarlet is anger, blue for love and yellow for jealousy.

Pedroline, the French version being Pierrot, also performed with this group of traveling players. His role was that of a simple minded and honest servant (zanni). Like Pedroline, Pierrot wears loose white garments with long sleeves and a neck ruffle, a soft-brimmed, floppy hat, large buttons down the front of the jacket and his face is whitened with powder like a clown's.

Columbine was a coy servant girl who originally wore a ballet dress and a wreath of roses while Pulcinello (the English version was Punchinello) eventually "outgrew" his mask and became a character in his own right.

The English version of the Commedia dell'arte was the Harlequinade which was performed in pantomine. Commedia dell'arte also influenced the Charlie Chaplin comedies, Marcel Marceau's mimes and the Punch and Judy show. Collectors will find a number of Noritake pieces decorated with these types of figures.

Novelty items seemed to be quite popular during the 20's and 30's. Some are referred to as figurines, some figurals and others flower frogs. Collectors often get confused as to just what constitutes each.

My interpretation is the following:

A figurine is a small molded figure or statuette with no moving parts. It has no utilitarian purpose but is merely decorative and ornamental. Some very famous ones that come to mind are the Hummel figurines, Boehm pieces and of course those from the Occupied Japan era.

A figural, although not found in the dictionary, is a popular term used by collectors. The dictionary does give us the word figure which means the visible form of anything and the suffix -al means pertains to or characterized by. Hence, the figural pertains to or is characterized by a figure in relief. Well known in the collecting field are the figural napkin rings decorated with attached birds or cherubs or squirrels, etc. in relief. There are also figural candy containers and figural bottles. All of these so-called figural items have a dual purpose. They have ornamentation in the shape of a figure but are also utilitarian as well as ornamental. It is my opinion then that figural pieces are those having either a relief figure attached for ornamentation to an utilitarian item or else the item is in the shape of a figure that is utilitarian by itself. For example, the glass bottles molded in the shape of a parrot or turtle that held alcoholic beverages or the old glass candy containers found in the shapes of soldiers, cars, etc. that held candy.

One also finds flower frogs or flower arrangers. They are often in the shape of a bird, tree stump, etc. with holes in the base to hold flowers. This provided a novel way to arrange one's cut flowers as the flower stems were inserted into the perforated base and the arranger was usually placed in a bowl of water.

If in doubt, it is always safe to classify all these types of items as novelties. Novelty means something unusual, also a small manufactured article and these items certaily do fall into this category. The old catalogs I have checked listed them as "novelty gift goods" so it seems to be an appropriate name to use even today.

During the Nippon era we find the RCA Nipper dog on the side of a pin dish. Other unique items are the owl and rabbit shaped lamps, the bird figurines, ashtrays decorated with dogs, birds, pipes and penguins in relief. There are also the figural two piece eggs molded in the shape of an egg of course, and used for trinkets, candy, etc. One will find relish dishes with a bird as the handle or a sardine dish with a sardine molded in relief as the finial. These items continued to be manufactured during the later Noritake years and old ads describe two-part dresser dolls that have space for a powder puff, trinkets or candy. There was also an elephant sitting on the side of an ashtray, a swan shaped serving dish, a sugar and creamer set in the form of ducks and fruit and flowers used as finials.

In this book you will find inkwells in the shapes of clowns and owls, ashtrays with sea nymphs, pipes, birds and clowns adorning them. There are wall vases decorated with birds and butterflies in relief, also celery dishes in the shapes of celery leaves. Flowers, fruit and birds were used for decorative finials and bridge ashtray sets came in the shape of hearts, diamond, clubs and spades. These unique items are a challenge to collect and are a "novel" addition to any collection.

Very popular with collectors are the Noritake items that are molded in relief or so-called "blown-out". These items are not actually blown-out as the term tends to indicate but this is a word used commonly by collectors and seems to pretty well describe the look of the item. The pattern gives the appearance of being raised as if there had been upward pressure from the underside. These pieces are not to be confused with those that simply have a heavy slip-trailing decoration added on after the item has been molded or those that have sprigged-on-decoration. These pieces have a three dimensional appearance and the pattern is made directly in the mold. Recesses were cut into the mold producing a negative relief. Whatever was incised into the mold would protrude out on the completed item. The design is raised up from the background of the item and is often found in the shape of nuts, flowers, animals, figures, etc. The figures and forms stand out from a flat surface and are raised above the background. The items are made in one piece although many look as though several pieces were used.

World Book Encyclopedia describes half relief decoration as being where the ornamentation stands out about half of its thickness and the figures are only partly molded. Some items are found in high relief where the figures or design project out more than half of their implied thickness while others are found in low relief where the decoration is just slightly raised and at times may be nearly as flat as that found on a coin.

The Noritake Co. tells me that Noritake's artists are given free rein to exercise their creative talents and it is safe to assume that this has been their policy through the years. The sketching and painting requires sophisticated hand painting skills and an artistic touch. I have been able to obtain a book from the Noritake Co. on the history of their company. Although it is written in Japanese the photos are self explanatory. In one photograph which is from the early 1900's there is a scene of an old decorating studio. There are long, low tables covered with a variety of pieces. All the decorators are sitting on the floor in typical Japanese fashion. There are about four people to a table with two on each side. The tables are covered with a variety of items, vases, ashtrays, hair receivers, etc. The photo shows about fifty decorators all in one area. The walls are windows much as our greenhouses are today and there appears to be racks to store the finished wares off to one side.

The matt colors used by Noritake's artists are soft and dull in appearance and look like velvet or suede when fired. A matt finish is not used for dinnerware as it absorbs dust and acids more readily. There seems to be two types of gold used with the overglaze, the bright gold that leaves a sheen and the one that fires dull and is then burnished to a satiny gold.

One of the most popular dinnerware patterns is the "white and gold". This particular pattern is still active with

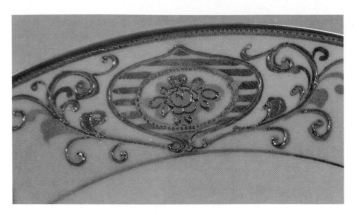

Close-up of white and gold pattern.

the Noritake Company and is in current stock in their United States warehouses. The shapes may be slightly different from the older pieces but the design appearance is the same. This pattern has survived many, many years and the Noritake Co. tells me that they feel "most affectionate and nostalgic about it as well as proud". They believe it is the only pre-war pattern that still exists in their line-up in today's market. According to the company, pattern D175 has been in production since 1912 and it remains a popular pattern all over the world even now. It was registered in Japan in 1930 and in the United States in 1950. The pattern appears to look like a Christmas ornament or perhaps an Oriental lantern. On the old tea cups the design is found on the outside, whereas it is now possible to purchase new tea cups with the design on either the inside or outside.

The first number used on these wares and listed on the backstamp is #16034 and was used during the Nippon era. Later, the number 43061 was used and it has been pointed out to me by collectors that this is merely the number 16034 written backwards. It is hard to believe this is merely a coincidence and since the Japanese read from right to left or just the opposite of us perhaps this explains why it was reversed at some point.

It is possible to collect this dinnerware bearing a number of backstamps and all seem to mix and match quite well. To date I have found pieces bearing backstamp #'s 12, 13, 29, 31, 35, 53, 54, 57, 58, 97 and the word "Japan" often appears on the salt and pepper shakers.

For those wishing to add new pieces to their old set, the Noritake Co. advises me that this pattern #175, white and gold, is presently designed in the La Salle shape and comes in the following pieces: cup, saucer, bread and butter plate, salad plate, dinner plate, soup, fruit, after dinner cup and saucer, three sizes of oval platters, large round vegetable bowl (salad bowl), oval vegetable (baker), covered vegetable, sugar with cover, creamer, coffee server with cover, teapot with cover, gravy with stand, covered butter, small round vegetable, salt and pepper, napkin ring, dinner bell, two tier tray and candle holder.

Collectors I have been in contact with report to me the following pre-war pieces that they have been able to collect in this patten. This is most likely an incomplete list and more items in this particular pattern probably exist. They have found two sizes of cups and saucers, evidently one is for tea and one for coffee, two sizes of gravies on attached plates, butter tub with insert (drain), creamer and sugar, teapot and cover, mayonnaise set consisting of an underplate, spoon and bowl (also referred to as a whip cream set), cracker or cookie jar, berry bowls, bread and butter plate, salad bowls, dinner plates, two sizes of open oval vegetables, a square open vegetable, 10″ tray, two sizes of relish dishes (8″ and 9½″), three sizes of platters (10″, 12″ and 14″), cereal bowls which are 7½″ in diameter, 6″ bowl, condiment set, butter dish with cover, 8½″ luncheon plates, fruit bowl, chocolate pot, demitasse size cups and saucers, spoon holder, four sizes of salt and peppers, a sectional dish, covered vegetables both round and oval, and a handled celery tray.

The Howo pattern is another that collectors are fond of. In 1903 William Griffis wrote the book *The Mikado's Empire*. In his chapter entitled "The mythical zoology of Japan" he describes a creature and says that its visits are rarer than those of angels, since it appears on the earth only at millennial intervals, or at the birth of some very great man.

"This fabulous bird, also of Chinese origin, is called the howo, or phenix. The tombs of the shoguns at Shiba and Nikko have most elaborate representations of the howo, and the new and old paper currency of the country bears it image. It seems to be a combination of the pheasant and peacock. A Chinese dictionary thus describes the fowl; "The phenix is of the essence of water; it was born in the vermillion cave; it roosts not but upon the most beautiful tree; it eats not but of the seeds of the bamboo; it drinks not but of the sweetest spring; its body is adorned with the Five Colors; its song contains the Five Notes; as it walks, it looks around; as it flies, the hosts of birds follow it". It has the head of a fowl, the crest of a swallow, the neck of a snake, the tail of a fish. Virtue, obedience, justice, fidelity, and benevolence are symbolized in the decorations on its head, wings, body, and breast".

"White & Gold" 9¾" dinner plate, mark #31; luncheon plate 8½" wide, mark #12. Fruit bowl, 5¼" wide, mark #57; spooner, 8½" long, mark #35.

"White & Gold" tea pot, 4¾" tall; sugar, 3¾" tall; creamer, 2½" tall, mark #35.

"White & Gold" bon bon dish, 6" square, mark #35.

"White & Gold", covered casserole dish, 13" long including handles.

Old "White & Gold" plate on left, new one on right. Note the differences in size & border.

"White & Gold" cake plate, 9¾" wide.

"New" tea cups in "White & Gold" pattern. Design can be ordered inside cup or outside.

Left to right: "White & Gold" demitasse cup, 2" tall, mark #31; salt shaker, 2½" tall, unmarked; salt shaker, 2-5/8" tall, mark #13; salt shaker, 1¾" tall, marked "Japan"; salt shaker, 3¾" tall, marked "Japan".

"Howo bird", covered jar, 5½" tall not including finial. Mark #55.

"Howo bird" covered jar, 5½" tall. Mark 16.

"Howo bird" demitasse set. Pot is 9" tall. Mark 55.

"Howo bird" cake plate, 9¾" wide. Mark 55.

"Howo bird" dinner plate, 10" wide. Mark 55.

59

Old Ads Featuring Noritake China

Tan & Gray Luster

E-6967—1 set in pkg........................Set **$1.95**
23-pc. set, light weight Japanese china, tan and gray luster, iris luster inside of cup and creamer, black hairline, hand painted bird on tree stump, natural color grass, half matt gold handles and knobs.

Tan & Cream Luster

E-9813—1 set in carton....................Set **$2.10**
23-pc. set, light weight Japanese china, tan & cream luster, cherry blossom and landscape design, solid luster spout on teapot, half matt gold handles and knobs, tan luster inside cup and creamer, black hairline.

Butler Bros. Catalog. August, 1929.

Blue Luster With Tan Luster Band

E-6965—1 set in pkg........................Set **$2.10**
23-pc. set, light weight Japanese china, blue luster ground with tan luster bands, and inner white shadow line giving fancy border effect, wild rose and green foliage decoration, luster handles, knobs and spout, iridescent luster inside cups.

3-Tone Color—Hand Painted

E-6968—1 set in pkg........................Set **$2.50**
23-pc. set, light weight Japanese china, 3-tone dark blue, ivory & light blue bands, bright **hand painted** floral and modernistic decoration, 2 black lines, luster handles, knobs and spout, iridescent luster inside cups

Tan & Ivory Luster—Hand Painted

E-6888—1 set in pkg........................Set **$3.25**
23-pc. set, light weight Japanese china, tan & ivory luster, **hand painted** floral decorations on black panels, luster knobs and handles, striped covers, mother-of-pearl luster inside cup and creamer.

Butler Bros. Catalog. December, 1931.

Jap China 23 Pc. Tea Set

Each set consists of 6 plates, 1 sugar (2 pcs.), 1 creamer, 6 cups, 6 saucers, 1 teapot (2 pcs.).

R6874—Lt. wt. Japanese china, double luster, **3 decorations,** (tan with blue bands, blue with tan bands, iris with mother-of-pearl bands), black inner line, solid color handles and knobs, contrasting luster inside cups and creamers. Asstd. 6 sets in case........SET (23 pcs) **$2.50**

100 PIECE JAPANESE CHINA DINNER SETS

"Elite"—Japanese china, trademarked, highly glazed, translucent, pink blossom clusters with green connecting vines on ⅜ in. ivory band, blue outlined lace border between tan hairline, inner gold hairlines, gold edges, half matte coin gold handles on all upright pieces. **No Package Charge.**

R31493—**100 piece set**—Shipping weight about 90 lbs. SET **$42.50**

"Parisian Border"—Japanese china, trademarked, first quality, light weight, pink, blue and green tinted medallions and rosebuds, with fancy ivory band, green, tan & blue scroll border, gold edges, half matte coin gold handles on all upright pieces. **No Package Charge.**

R31893—**100 piece set**—Shipping weight about 00 lbs. SET (100 pcs) **$56.00**

"Laurelton"—Japanese china, light weight, extra fine quality, blue & green laurel wreath on ivory tinted ground, blue lattice border, delft blue & pink rose medallions, gold edges and half matte coin gold handles and knobs. **No Package Charge.**

R31093—**100 piece set**—Shipping weight about 90 lbs. SET (100 pcs) **$52.00**

Butler Bros. Catalog. June, 1924.

23-Piece Imported China Tea-Set

Beautiful set of fine, white imported china, decorated in the popular style with blue lustre band set off with medallions of flowers in bright colors. Consists of teapot of 5-cup capacity, sugar bowl, cream pitcher, 6 standard-size teacups and saucers and 6 plates. 7¼ in. in diameter. Shpg. wt. 10 lbs.

4871 With **$10** *Purchase or Coupons*

Larkin Catalog. Fall/Winter, 1927.

"PAISLEY"—Noritake

(McDonald Bros. No. A6100)

Fine quality, light weight china, clear white glaze, Paisley border designs with gold rim, blue, green and yellow floral sprays on rim, inner gold line, floral and fruit center spray on plates, half matte gold knobs and handles. **No package charge.**

Dinner Sets

R21896—50 pc. set.	Ship. wt. abt. 50 lbs.....	Set	Temp.
R21891—97 "	" " " " 90 " .... "		Out

Open Stock

R21800—Cup 3¾x2, saucer 5½ in....	DOZ (24 pcs)	**$8.30**
R21807—Boullion 3⅝x2, saucer 5½ in.	" "	**11.89**
R21808—After dinner coffee cup & saucer	" "	**6.75**
R21810—Plate, b. & b., actual 6⅜ in.........	Doz	**3.50**
R21812— " tea, actual 7½ in......	"	**5.70**
R21813— " breakfast, actual 8½ in......	"	**7.50**
R21814— " dinner, actual 9¾ in..........	"	**T. O.**
R21817— " coupe soup, actual 7⅜ in......	"	**7.50**
R21845—Platter, actual 11½ in.............	Each	**2.00**
R21847— " " 13¾ "	"	**2.40**
R21848— " " 16 "	"	**3.50**
R21825—Baker, actual 10½ in.............	"	**1.85**
R21853—Salad, actual 9¾ in..............	"	**1.95**
R21860—Fruit dish, actual 5¼ in.........	Doz	**3.30**
R21865—Oatmeal, actual 5¾ in............	"	**4.80**
R21876—Creamer, 3¼ in. high............	Each	**1.00**
R21877—Sugar, 4 in. high.................	"	**1.70**
R21883—Casserole, actual 8½ in...........	"	**4.25**
R21884—Sauce boat, fast stand...........	"	**2.00**
R21886—Pickie dish, actual 8¼ in.........	"	**.85**
R21887—Tea pot, cap. six cups.............	"	**2.50**

Butler Bros. Catalog. August, 1928.

NORITAKE CHINA TEA SET

This beautiful, imported tea set of white china is made appealing by the narrow border decoration in light blue and orange on an ivory background. Artistic sprays of flowers in pink, blue and orange, with green foliage, add further charm. Edges and handles trimmed in gold. Consists of a tea pot of five-cup capacity, covered sugar bowl, cream pitcher, six standard-size tea cups, six saucers and six plates 7¼ in. in diameter. Shpg. wt. 18 lbs.

2386 With **$10** *Purchase or Coupons*

Larkin Catalog. Spring/Summer, 1932.

"GLENORA"—Noritake

(McDonald Bros. No. A5300)

Fine quality light weight pure white china, variegated colors, blue, green, rose and black medallions set on ivory border circumscribed by black lines, gold line edge, half matte gold handles and knobs. **No package charge.**

Dinner Sets

R21696— 50 pc. set. Ship. wt. abt. 50 lbs....Set **$24.32**
R21693—100 "   "   "   "   " 90 " ... " **49.60**

Open Stock

R21600—Cup 3¾x2, saucer 5½ in....DOZ (24 pcs) **$5.25**
R21607—Boullion 3⅝x2, saucer 5½ in. " /24 ") **8.00**
R21608—After dinner coffee cup & saucer " (24 ") **5.25**
R21620—Cream soup 5x1¾, saucer 6¾ " (24 ") **16.00**
R21610—Plate, b. & b., actual 6⅜ in.........Doz **3.25**
R21612— " tea, actual 7½ in............ " **4.95**
R21613— " breakfast, actual 8½ in...... " **6.75**
R21614— " dinner, actual 9¾ in.......... " **7.75**
R21617— " coupe soup, actual 7⅜ in..... " **6.00**
R21618— " cake, actual 9⅝ in..........Each **1.50**
R21643—Platter, actual 10 in.............. " **1.25**
R21645— " " 11⅝ " .... " **1.80**
R21647— " " 13¾ " .... " **2.50**
R21648— " " 16 " .... " **3.50**
R21624—Baker, actual 9½ in.............. " **1.25**
R21625— " " 10½ " .... " **1.55**
R21653—Salad, actual 9⅞ in............... " **1.50**
R21660—Fruit dish, actual 5¼ in.........Doz **2.85**
R21665—Oatmeal, actual 5⅝ in............. " **4.00**
R21676—Creamer, 3¼ in. high.........Each **.75**
R21677—Sugar, 4 in. high................. " **1.25**
R21678—Covered butter, actual 7¼ in....... " Out
R21683—Casserole, actual 8½ in.......... " **3.25**
R21684—Sauce boat, fast stand........... " **1.75**
R21686—Pickle dish, actual 8¼ in. .... " Out
R21687—Tea pot, cap. six cups........... " **2.00**

"BANCROFT"—Noritake

(McDonald Bros. No. A4300)

Light weight china, clear white glaze, conventional black and tan border with inner ivory band, broken by yellow and tan conventional medallions. **No package charge.**

Dinner Sets

R21296—50 pc. set. Ship. wt. abt. 50 lbs.....Set **$27.75**
R21291—97 " "   "   "   " 90 " .... " **53.20**

Open Stock

R21200—Cup 3¾x2, saucer 5½ ir ....DOZ (24 pcs) **$7.80**
R21207—Boullion 3⅝x2, saucer 5½ in. " " **10.00**
R21220—Cream soup 5x1¾, saucer 6¾ " " **15.00**
R21210—Plate, b. & b., actual 6⅜ in.........Doz **3.10**
R21212— " pie, actual 7½ in............ " **5.05**
R21213— " breakfast, actual 8½ in...... " **6.75**
R21214— " dinner, actual 9¾ in.......... " **8.00**
R21217— " coupe soup, actual 7⅜ in...... " **6.75**
R21245—Platter, actual 11⅝ in.............Each **1.80**
R21247— " " 13½ " .... " **2.10**
R21248— " " 15¾ " .... " **3.20**
R21225—Baker, actual 10½ in.............. " **1.75**
R21253—Salad, actual 9⅞ in................ " **1.75**
R21260—Fruit dish, actual 5¼ in.............Doz **3.00**
R21265—Oatmeal, actual 5⅝ in............. " **5.00**
R21276—Creamer, 3¼ in. high.............Each **.85**
R21277—Sugar, 4 in. high................. " **1.60**
R21283—Casserole, actual 8½ in............ " **3.85**
R21284—Sauce boat, fast stand............. " **1.90**
R21286—Pickle dish, actual 8¼ in. .... " **.70**
R21287—Tea pot, cap. six cups............... " **2.00**

Butler Bros. Catalog. August, 1928.

Tan & Blue Luster

E-6966—1 set in pkg........................Set **$2.10**
23-pc. set, light weight Japanese china, tan & blue luster, Japanese scenic decoration, luster handles, knobs and spout.

Tan & Blue Luster—Decorated

E-6880—1 set in pkg........................Set **$2.7**
23-pc. set, light weight Japanese china, tan & blue luster floral decoration, black lines, luster handles and knobs mother-of-pearl luster inside cup.

Butler Bros. Catalog. December, 1931.

2-Tone Tintings—Hand Painted ☞

E-6925—1 set in carton.....................**Set $5.00**
23-pc. set, light weight Japanese china, Japanese landscape design in 2-tone tintings, **hand painted** floral decorations, coin gold stems, dark green band with fancy scroll design in coin gold between gold bands, coin gold half matt handles and knobs, iridescent luster inside cup and creamer.

Butler Bros. Catalog. December, 1931.

"MALVERN"—Noritake

(Mc Donald Bros. No. A5400)

First quality light weight china, clear white glaze, variegated floral medallion with blue scroll, gold line on edge, wide ivory border outlined by black and yellow bands, half matte gold handles and knobs. **No package charge.**

Dinner Sets

R21796— 50 pc. set. Ship. wt. abt. 50 lbs....Set	$29.95
R21791— 97 " " " " " 90 " ... "	58.00

Open Stock

R21700—Cup 3¾x2, saucer 5½ in....DOZ (24 pcs)	$8.39
R21707—Boullion 3⅝x2, saucer 5½ in. " "	11.37
R21708—After dinner coffee cup & saucer " "	6.48
R21720—Cream soup 5x1¾, saucer 6¾ " "	17.00
R21710—Plate, b. & b., actual 6⅜ in..........Doz	3.50
R21712— " tea, actual 7½ in............. "	5.87
R21713— " breakfast, actual 8½ in....... "	7.69
R21714— " dinner, actual 9¾ in.......... "	8.88
R21717— " coupe soup.................. "	7.69
R21745—Platter, actual 11⅝ in..............Each	1.89
R21747— " " 13½ "............. "	2.48
R21748— " " 15¾ "............. "	3.69
R21725—Baker, actual 10½ in................ "	1.89
R21753—Salad, actual 9⅞ in................. "	1.89
R21760—Fruit dish, actual 5¼ in............Doz	3.38
R21765—Oatmeal, actual 5⅝ in............... "	4.98
R21776—Creamer, 3¼ in. high..............Each	.96
R21777—Sugar, 4 in. high................... "	1.59
R21783—Casserole, actual 8½ in............. "	3.98
R21784—Sauce boat, fast stand.............. "	2.18
R21786—Pickle dish, actual 8¼ in........... "	.76
R21787—Tea pot, cap. six cups.............. "	2.25

"MAYFAIR"—Noritake

(McDonald Bros. No. A6500)

Fine quality light weight china, clear white glaze, gold band on rim, diamond checked tan and blue band, ivory border broken by rose wreaths and green floral medallions. **No package charge.**

Dinner Sets

R22096—50 pc. set. Ship. wt. abt. 50 lbs.......Set	Temp.
R22091—97 " " " " " 90 " ...... "	Out

Open Stock

R22000—Cup 3¾x2, saucer 5½ in....DOZ (24 pcs)	$8.75
R22007—Bouillon cup and saucer..... " "	12.00
R22020—Cream soup cup and saucer.. " "	20.00
R22010—Plate, b. & b., actual 6⅜ in..........Doz	3.60
R22012— " tea, actual 7½ in............. "	6.00
R22013— " breakfast, actual 8½ in....... "	8.00
R22014— " dinner, actual 9¾ in.......... "	T. O.
R22017— " coupe soup, actual 7⅜ in..... "	8.00
R22018— " cake, actual 9⅝ in...........Each	1.75
R22045—Platter, actual 11⅝ in.............. "	2.00
R22047— " " 13½ "............. "	2.50
R22048— " " 15¾ "............. "	3.75
R22025—Baker, actual 10½ in................ "	2.00
R22053—Salad, actual 9⅞ in................. "	2.00
R22060—Fruit dish, actual 5¼ in............Doz	3.50
R22076—Creamer, 3¼ in. high..............Each	1.00
R22077—Sugar, 4 in. high................... "	1.75
R22083—Casserole, actual 8½ in............. "	Temp.
R22084—Sauce boat, fast stand.............. "	Out
R22086—Pickle dish, actual 8¼ in........... "	.75
R22087—Tea pot, cap. six cups.............. "	2.75

Butler Bros. Catalog. August, 1928.

23-Piece Noritaké China Tea-Set

1102 With $12 *Purchase or Coupons*

Beautiful set of fine, white imported china, decorated in the popular style with blue luster band set off with medallions of flowers in bright colors. Consists of teapot of 5-cup capacity, sugar bowl, cream pitcher, 6 standard-size teacups and saucers and 6 plates, 7⅝ in. in diameter. Shpg. wt. 10 lbs.

Larkin Catalog. Fall/Winter, 1926-27.

Imported Genuine China Dinner Sets

OUTSTANDING VALUES—JAPANESE MADE—SEE PAGE 363 FOR COMPOSITION OF DINNERWARE SETS

105-Piece Set in Lovely Floral Pattern
Clear white china with attractive floral decorations in rose and blue on wide cream border with tan and light pale green trim.
55R-9632—1 set in carton, 85 lbs.......Set $24.75 105 Pcs.

93-Piece Set with Floral Border
Clear white china, wide cream border with painted flower design and gold edging. All the handles are trimmed with gold, too.
55R-9635—1 set in carton, 75 lbs.......Set $19.80 93 Pcs.

93-Piece Set with Appealing Floral Pattern
Clear white china with tan trimmed wide cream border. The floral design is red tinted and there's a gold edge.
55R-9630—1 set in carton, 75 lbs.....Set $21.00 93 Pcs.

Our Top Quality 93-Piece Set
High grade white china with wide cream border trimmed with blue floral design, gold edging, half matt handles.
55R-9633—1 set in carton, 75 lbs......Set $24.75 93 Pcs.

53-Piece China Dinner Sets
Predominantly maroon trim, china white body, cream colored pastel border with natural color flower sprays, gold edge. This snowy white china with its beautiful design and expensive looking hand painted decorations is a real buy at its price. Made in Japan. For composition of sets see the chart on a nearby page.
55R-9637—1 set in carton, 40 lbs..............Set 9.50

53-Piece China Dinner Sets
Predominantly blue trim, china white body, cream colored pastel border with natural color wild flower pattern, gold edged. Japanese made. This set is also a real value in genuine imported China . . . represents values that mean savings and selling opportunities for you. Order now while sets are still available.
55R-9636—1 set in carton, 40 lbs Set 9.50

Butler Bros. Catalog. Fall, 1941.

High Grade 53-Piece China Dinner Sets
A special value in high grade decorated china . . . worth more than the price. Wide ivory border, trimmed in gold with blue floral decal decorations, on clear white, thin, lightweight china . . . attractive from every aspect. Made in Japan. For composition of sets see the chart on a nearby page.
55R-9634—1 set in carton, 40 lbs............Set **13.50**

93-Piece China Dinner Sets
Wide cream border with hand painted border of garland of roses and wild flowers, inner fancy scroll border with fancy edge border of tan and gray figures, gold edges, half matt handles and knobs, gold treated platter, all pieces light weight. Japanese made. Beautifully hand painted and attractively designed.
55R-9624—1 set in pkg, 75 lbs...............Set **22.50**

**Butler Bros. Catalog.
Fall, 1941.**

After Dinner Imported China Cups & Saucers

R5085—Lt. wt. white china, tinted gold stamped floral medallion and scroll, gold edges, inner hairline, striped handle, cup 3⅞x2, saucer 5½ in. 2 doz. in pkg.
DOZ (24 pcs) $1.35
30 doz. or more, Doz **1.28**

R5028—Japanese design, Tokio red edges and red traced handles, cup 2⅛x2⅛, saucer 4¼ in. 2 doz. in pkg.
DOZ (24 pcs) 84c
12 doz. or more, Doz **82c**
48 doz. or more, Doz **78c**

R5047—Double luster china, rich tan and blue combination, black hairline, tan luster inside, blue handle, cup 3¾x2, saucer 5½ in. 2 doz. in pkg.
DOZ (24 pcs) ★1.68

R5031—Gold edges and handle, cup 2⅛x2¼, saucer 4⅜ in. 2 doz. in pkg.
DOZ (24 pcs) 84c
12 doz. or more, Doz **82c**
48 doz. or more, Doz **78c**

Butler Bros. Catalog. August, 1928.

Lowest Price Yet!

Jap China Cup & Saucer

TWO-TONE LUSTER

Jap china has gone up during the last 60 days 15% to 20%. Yet, this is a lower price than we could name a year ago. Think what a value this is.

R5047—Double luster china, rich tan and blue combination, black hairline, tan luster inside, blue handle. Cup 3¾x2, saucer 5½ in. 2 doz. in pkg—no package charge.
DOZ (24 pcs) **$1.68**

Butler Bros. Catalog. August, 1928.

Imported China Dinner Sets
Beautifully shaped pieces, charmingly decorated with conventional ivory border design with dark blue medallions, interspersed with sprays of pink flowers and green leaves; edges and handles traced with bright gold.

Hollywood 52-pc. Set 2510 **$55** *With* Purchase or Coupons Shpg. wt. 56 lbs.
Composition of Set: Six each: Dinner plates, tea plates, bread-and-butter plates, fruit saucers, soup plates, cups and saucers. One each: Platter, salad bowl, gravy-boat (with stand attached), covered vegetable dish, sugar bowl, cream pitcher and open vegetable dish.

Hollywood 100-pc. Set 2516 **$95** *With* Purchase or Coupons Shpg. wt. 98 lbs.
Composition of Set: Twelve each: Dinner plates, tea plates, bread-and-butter plates, soup plates, fruit saucers, cups and saucers. One each: Platter (11 in.), platter (13 in.), covered vegetable dish, casserole, gravy-boat (with stand attached), open vegetable dish, pickle dish, sugar bowl, cream pitcher and covered butter dish with drainer.

INDIVIDUAL OFFERS

Set of Six,	No.	With Purchase	Size in.	Mlg. Wt. lbs.	One of each,	No.	With Purchase	Size in.	Mlg. Wt. lbs.
Dinner Plates	2518	$9.00	10	6	Sugar & Cream Set	2554	$4.00		1½
Tea Plates	2525	4.50	7½	3½	Pickle Dish	2578	1.80		12 oz.
Br. & Bu. Plates	2527	3.50	6	2	Gravy Boat	2563	4.00		1¾
Soup Plates	2536	6.50	7¾	4½	Casserole	2555	6.50		2¾
Fruit Saucers	2539	3.30	5½	2	Vegetable Dish	2589	3.00		2
Oatmeal Dishes	2540	4.50	5¾	2	Covered Dish	2592	6.50		3¼
Cups & Saucers	2541	6.50		4	Salad Bowl	2557	2.50	9½	2¼
One of each,					Cake Plate	2559	2.50	9½	2½
Medium Platter	2547	4.00	13	2½	Butter Dish	2594	2.60		1¾
Small Platter	2542	3.20	11½	1¾	Teapot	2560	3.40	5 cup	2¾

Larkin Catalog. Fall/Winter, 1927-28.

PLEASE NOTE: Our prices on cups and saucers include both pieces—24 pieces to dozen except where otherwise stated.

Tan and Gold Decorated
China, floral spray, wide cream luster band decorated in tan with gold edge, gold traced cup handle. Japanese made.
55-7004—2 doz in carton ....Doz **1.72**

Floral Spray with Bands
China, gold traced cup handle. Japanese made. 2 doz in carton.
55-7000—Red banded
55-7001—Blue banded
55-7002—Green banded
Doz **1.75**

Green and Gold Decorated
China, floral spray, wide cream luster band decorated in green with gold edge, gold traced cup handle. Japanese made.
55-7003—2 doz in carton..........Doz **1.80**

Butler Bros. Catalog. Fall, 1941.

Matching Services For Noritake

There are several well known and reputable dealers that specialize in matching Noritake dinnerware sets. Their names and addresses are found in the antique trade papers and magazines.

Most have hundreds of patterns in their warehouses. They recommend that you send either a good clear photo, a photostatic copy of a small dish or saucer or preferably the saucer itself. Many keep on hand what they refer to as their saucer file. A SASE (self-addressed, stamped envelope) is also required for a reply.

A number of the dinnerware pieces have pattern numbers or names printed on the bottom but this is not enough when trying to locate matching pieces for your set. The pattern names and numbers changed after World War II and just because the name is the same does not mean that the pattern is always the same.

So that there are no mistakes in matching up your dinnerware set, it is necessary for the matching service to have a record on file for you. If they do not have a particular item in stock, most will keep your name on file and notify you if and when they do locate the pattern. Some old patterns have no name or number backstamped on them and it seems to me that it must be an awesome job

for these people keeping them all straight in their minds and which one is which. Of course, they also buy as well as sell, so if you have extras of dinnerware pieces that you would like to sell drop them a line describing what you have. There are variances in pricing but the more popular patterns such as the Azalea or the Tree in the Meadow generally command a higher price. This also works in the reverse. So if you are buying you can expect to pay more for certain patterns.

Peggy Rousch operates a matching service for Noritake pieces and was kind enough to send me the following 84 saucers so that they could be photographed and included in the book. To date she has been unable to identify these patterns and as an aid to collectors I have assigned a number to each so that they may refer to this when locating extra pieces. All 84 saucers do not necessarily fall into the 1921-41 time period covered in this book. The backstamp will guide you as to the year of manufacture. Some are from the Nippon era and some date after 1941 but all have been included as a help to collectors. I have preceeded each saucer with the letters NP which stand for Noritake Pattern.

NP-1 unmarked

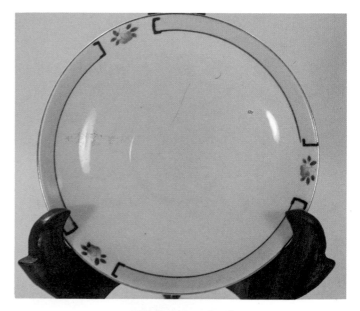

NP-2 unmarked

NP-3 unmarked

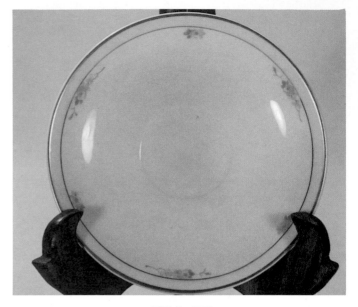

NP-4 #23

NP-5 #23

NP-6 #28

NP-7 unmarked

NP-8 unmarked

NP-9 #23

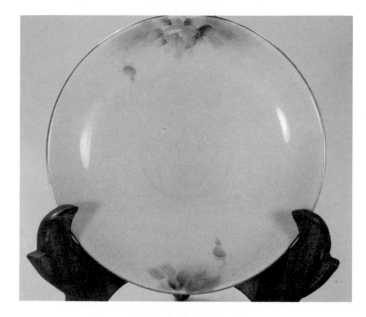

NP-10 unmarked

NP-11 unmarked

NP-12 unmarked

NP-13 unmarked

NP-14 #23

NP-15 #87

NP-16 unmarked

NP-17 #50

NP-18 #89

NP-19 #50

NP-20 #50

NP-21 #50

NP-22 #50

NP-23 #50

NP-24 #50

NP-25 #22

NP-26 #89

NP-27 #50

NP-28 #87

NP-29 #87

NP-30 #91

NP-31 #73

NP-32 #79

70

NP-33 #22

NP-34 #81

NP-35 #50

NP-36 unmarked

NP-37 #35

NP-38 #63

NP-39 #28

NP-40 #79

NP-41 #81

NP-42 #79

NP-43 #81

NP-44 #87

NP-45 #81

NP-46 #73

NP-47 #88

NP-48 #73

NP-49 #88

NP-50 #87

NP-51 #95

NP-52 #73

NP-53 #73

NP-54 #91

NP-55 #72

NP-56 #72

NP-57 #72

NP-58 #50

NP-59 #73

NP-60 #50

NP-61 #73

NP-62 #52

NP-63 #73

NP-64 #81

NP-65 #73

NP-66 #73

NP-67 #73

NP-68 #91

NP-69 #73

NP-70 #79

NP-71 #73

NP-72 #73

NP-73 #73

NP-74 #73

NP-75 #50

NP-76 #87

NP-77 #73

NP-78 #73

NP-79 #50

NP-80 #73

NP-81 #73

NP-82 #16

NP-83 #16

NP-84 #96

Other Items With Unidentifiable Patterns

NP #85-plate is 7½″ wide, sugar bowl is 6″ wide, creamer is 3½″ tall, and bowl is 7¼″ wide. All have mark #73.

NP #86-individual teapot, 6½″ tall, mark #27.

NP #87-plate, 9¾″ wide; gravy, 9½″ long, mark #27.

NP #88-set of cake plates, 6½″ wide, mark #27.

NP #89-plate, 8½″ wide, mark #27.

NP #90-fruit dish, mark #27.

NP #91-covered dish with underplate, 5″ long, mark #27.

NP #92-demitasse cup and saucer, mark #16.

NP #93-demitasse cup and saucer, mark #39.

Identifiable Patterns and Mark

Daventry #42.

Winona #47.

Ashby #62.

Eltovar #61.

Floreal #48.

Homeric #70.

Amesbury #36.

Belvoir #68.

Lancashire #41.

Berenda #69.

Roseara #46.

All pieces in dinner set "The Vitry," mark #24.

Grasmere #45.

Grasmere #45.

Irvington #60.

Irvington #60.

Lynbrook #71.

Goldcraft #51.

The Art of Entertaining Correctly in the 20's and 30's

Over the years there has been a gradual development in the art of entertaining and serving food correctly, from simple to elaborate, from eating out of handmade clay bowls to the elegant formal dining of the Victorian period. During the turn of the century period there were so many dishes on the table it's a wonder there was room for any food. Beginning in 1921, following World War I, there was an air of lightheartedness and the Art Deco period swept the country.

A spectacular boom occurred. Materialism flourished. America craved excitement and a free wheeling mood hit the decade. "Eat, drink and be merry" is the axiom that best sums up the feeling of the time. Racketeering was widespread probably due to the Prohibition laws. Instead of putting a stop to the drinking it seemed to have the reverse effect and Americans drank more than usual. Speakeasies sprang up all over.

By 1928, however, the prices of stocks had soared beyond the point of a safe return and then the unthinkable happened. The market collapsed! The Great Depression gripped the country for twelve years and the pleasures and frivolities that had been taken for granted only a few years earlier were now gone.

The thirties were the "lean years". Unemployment was up to 25% at one period and on March 4th, 1933 the banking system of the United States collapsed.

The country gradually got itself back on its feet and by 1939 the gross national profit had climbed more than 60% over that of 1933. In 1939 the German tanks also rolled into Poland and it became the beginning of World War II.

The Art Deco style prevailed in the 20's and 30's and was one of highly stylized designs, bright colors and geometric shapes. In this period, cubist painting was fashionable, also zig-zag designs and expressionism. The style was influenced by the art of the ancient Egyptians and Romans, also that of the Mexican Incas and the American Indian. The Noritake china imported into the United States at this time also underwent changes that reflected this new life style.

The old catalogs give us a clue as to what was popular during this time period. A 1927 Larkin catalog displays a dresser set consisting of a compact powder box decorated with a Colonial dame in purple dress holding a black fan. The matching pin tray is decorated with the figural of a dog. There is a jam jar, it is solid blue luster with a bright red apple serving as the finial. There are flower holders in the shapes of birds, china wall pockets for displaying decorative flowers, honey jars in the shape of beehives and dresser dolls for powder puffs, trinkets, candy, etc.

During these years there was a profusion of dishes available, they came in all shapes and sizes. There were vases to match dinnerware sets, berry sugar and cream sets, whipped cream sets, egg cups, mustard jars, butter tubs, lemon sets, individual salt and pepper shakers, comports, spoon holders, butter chips, the list goes on and on.

In just the Azalea pattern, one had a choice of six sizes of plates, there was a 6½″ size bread and butter, a 7½″ tea plate, a 7-5/8″ square fruit or salad plate, a 8½″ breakfast plate, a 9¾″ dinner plate and the 10¼″ grill plate. In this same pattern were four sizes of platters, a 10½″, 12″, 14″, and 16″. Over the years the Noritake Company offered 69 different items for sale in this pattern including salad bowls, condiment sets, teapots, gravy bowls, syrup pitchers, egg cups, etc.

Next to an ad for salt dip sets are the words "The thoughtful hostess provides individual open salt dishes". Ashtrays were "grooved for cigars". One finds that toothpick holders were usually described as being interchangeable with match holders. One salt and pepper shaker set was in the shape of a "quaint little girl pepper shaker and the open salt dish in the shape of a swan with a salt spoon on an oval tray". Talcum powder shakers were offered in the fall 1927 Larkin catalog in the shape of a doll. Vanity sets consisted of a Dresden lady figure which formed the stopper of the perfume bottle and one became the cover of the powder box.

The novelty pieces and figurals are a favorite with collectors. Who can resist the adorable cat sitting atop a powder box or the bird used as a finial on a relish dish? These seem to be indicative of the Art Deco era and are more readily found than those made in the Nippon era.

Bowls were formed in the shape of nuts, asparagus sets in the shape of asparagus and corn sets in the shapes of ears of corn.

In the old Butler Bros. catalogs of the twenties, knickers were featured for both men and women, middy blouses were a hit with the ladies, collar pins and buttons in assorted styles were offered including the "Kum-a-part-

Kuff Buttons". Shaving mugs were still popular as well as cuspidors. In 1928 the rage was games such as *Moon Mullins Game, Little Orphan Annie Game* and the *Toonerville Trolley*. They sold for $7.50 a dozen. One could purchase a map balloon which still seems like a novel idea. It was described as "a balloon with educational features, complete world map permanently printed on rubber showing all countries of the world, principal cities and rivers". They were 32″ in circumference and could be purchased at 12 for 72ᶜ.

By 1933 Butler Bros. was featuring Mickey Mouse watches and Babe Ruth knives. There was also "phantom red" and "kissproof" rouge for the ladies. Glass sipper spoons were offered in the old catalogs. They were "long hollow crystal tube handles with colored spoons on the ends".

What were ordinary dishes to the people of this time period would be extraordinary to us. I don't use a jam jar or mustard jar, egg warmers would look out of place at my house. I also don't use butter chips or china wall pockets. The years have brought changes in our dining manners and habits but it is so interesting to know how our forefathers entertained. Collecting is enhanced by learning and the past enriches the present. Our "roots" can be traced through our old dishes and this heritage can then be passed onto our children and grandchildren.

How To Care For Your Noritake Porcelain

Wash your items carefully, do not put a lot of items in the sink at one time. Use softened water if possible for both the washing and rinsing. The dishwater should only be as hot as your hands can bear and the rinse water should be about the same temperature. Use a mild detergent and never, never use abrasives or scouring pads as this will often wear off some of the decoration. If an item is real dirty, a good long soaking in water and soap will usually correct the problem. If not, take a stiff bottle brush for scrubbing those hard to reach places. Tea and coffee stains should be taken care of immediately.

Don't use chlorine bleach on your hand painted items. Discolored hairlines can sometimes be cleaned with a dab of chlorine on a cotton swab but never immerse the whole article in it. Hairlines may disappear temporarily but it is not a permanent solution to the problem. Some authorities believe that cracks can be boiled clean, however, I would not subject my pieces to great changes in temperature.

Don't leave items out where they can get knocked over or accidently hit. Keep them out of the reach of small children and family pets. Stop accidents before they happen.

When storing your dishes, separate them with napkins, paper, felt, doilies, etc. Items that are unglazed on the bottom may not only scratch each other but furniture as well so it would be advisable to be careful when placing these pieces on your wooden or glass furniture.

Cups should not be stacked on top of one another as there is always the risk of chipping. Also don't hang them by their handles as this is their weakest point.

If you store items in boxes or are packing them to be mailed, be sure to wrap them well. Do not use newspaper as the newsprint can rub off on the piece. Disposable diapers or hospital pads make good wrappers and provide adequate protection. When mailing items, a good suggestion would be to use these wrappers plus foam chips and double box your pieces. After wrapping the items, newspaper can be rolled up and placed in the box as a filler.

Try to buy the best you can afford. Check to see that the item is free of cracks, hairlines, etc. Pieces in "mint" condition are always in demand and should continue to increase in value for you.

Detection of Damage and Restoration

Ever get an item home only to discover a crack or hairline? Most of us are quick to buy and quick to trust when the person offering the piece tells us it is in "mint condition".

LOOKING BEFORE YOU LEAP is good advice. Buy quality and always buy the best you can afford for these items will hold their value. Knowingly buying damaged or restored items is a matter that should be left to each collector's judgment. It's rare that these pieces will escalate in value and such purchases should probably be avoided unless the article is extremely rare or very, very cheap. However, there is really nothing wrong in buying either as long as it is always identified as such and not misrepresented.

Know your dealer or else be very careful with your purchase. Never buy an item under poor lighting conditions, always hold the piece up to the light. You can often tell by touching the items if something is wrong. Check the most vulnerable places, areas that project, such as spouts, handles, rims, sprigged-on decoration, etc.

Gold wears off the quickest because it is the last to be fired and it is quite common to find touched-up gold. It is often duller than the original and this fact can often detect its presence. Droplets of color are another tell-tale clue along with pieces of lint or hair which would never have survived firing in the kiln. Check to see if there are any conspicuous areas of dull coloring where surrounding areas are shiny and vice versa. Anyone can be an innocent buyer and be fooled.

Some collectors have approached the problem of detecting hidden damage with the purchase of a long wave ultraviolet light. It can be a valuable aid in the detection of *most* repairs. When viewed under black light, hard to see cracks will fluoresce brightly. And then there are still those who advertise restorations that are invisible under black light. It can really make a collector leary.

(Used with permission of Collector Books. Excerpt from *The Collector's Encyclopedia of Nippon Porcelain*, Series II by Joan F. Van Patten.)

Recording and Insuring Your Collection

One thing every serious collector should do is keep accurate records on all items. This can be just for your own pleasure but more realistically as a help in case of fire or theft. Three sets should be kept, one at home, one in a safety deposit box and one with your insurance company.

These records can either be kept in book form or perhaps a filing card system could be utilized. Several books for this purpose are already on the market and should be considered by collectors. Photos are a must! Along with these one should list the date and place the item was acquired, original cost and its physical description such as height, width, diameter, etc. Condition should be noted, example: mint, chipped, worn gold, hairlines. The identifying mark should also be jotted down along with the current value of the item. These records should be updated yearly.

Insurance costs always seem to be on the rise as is the possibility of theft. One solution for the collector would be to contain the collection to one that is small and choice.

Easy to say, hard to do, so if you are like most who have been bitten by the collecting bug contact your insurance company as to the possibility of obtaining a fine arts policy. It is a rider to the homeowner's policy and since insurance laws vary from state to state it would be advisable to speak with your local agent. Insure the items for their full value. Any new increases in value are not covered so amend your policy periodically. Household accidents such as breakage are not included however.

No one likes to think about thefts and fires but they do occur. First of all do not advertise the existence of your collection to everyone you meet. Good locks on doors and windows are a first step while many other collectors have preferred to install alarm systems. Check with your insurance company as these installations may give you a break on your premium.

(An excerpt from *The Collector's Encyclopedia of Nippon Porcelain, Series II* by Joan F. Van Patten, used with permission of Collector Books.)

Backstamps

The majority of the backstamps shown are actual photographs that the Noritake Co. has supplied or that I was able to obtain from my items. The others are hand drawn facsimiles of marks submitted by the Company or collectors who have tried to help us in our quest for knowledge.

The Noritake Co. did not realize how important the dating of these pieces would be to collectors in later years and regretfully they do not have information regarding many of their marks. They are not sure of many cut-off dates or when one mark started and another was discontinued. They believe the letter M appeared in their backstamps until the letter N was registered in 1953. The American occupation of Japan lasted until 1952 when "Occupied Japan" should also have been placed on the wares. In 1953 they started using the N.

According to the Noritake Co., the designs and shapes of most of their wares were European preferred and were for the Western taste. They assume that their old marks have the English backstamps on them even for the domestic market in Japan because they never possessed a Japanese written backstamp until about ten years ago when they started manufacturing authentic Japanese wares. In Japan, many manufacturers adopted the English spelling of brand names for their commodity even for the domestic market.

The Noritake Co. does not know nor can they guess how the pattern numbers were assigned. These are found in many of the backstamps.

The Company was only required to have the country of origin on their items and naturally added their own logo as they were very proud of the wares they had produced. I have tried to date the pieces as carefully as possible with the company's help and also relying upon old catalogs and brochures.

Most of the infomation regarding the dating of backstamps has been gathered at a slow pace and at times it has almost been like pulling teeth. Some was gleaned from the old catalogs, some from collectors, some from my own collection and the majority from the Noritake Co. In many cases we can date the beginning year of manufacture for items with a particular backstamp but not when it ended. Obviously anything with "Nippon" printed in the backstamp as country of origin dates back to an earlier period and those with "Occupied Japan" date after World War II until 1952. Marks having a N in them date from 1953 on. Some marks can only be guessed at as to the

time period. New information is surfacing all the time and I am sure there will be many corrections and additions made to this listing over the years but as it now stands is a guideline and the best that we have available. I have tried to be as accurate as possible and only wish it were a more complete list. Hopefully future researchers and historians may be able to elaborate on this information.

Morimura Brothers Era, 1878-1884. There are records that during this period Morimura Brothers had their own decoration kiln in Japan but what backstamp they used is unknown.

1884-1890. In 1882, Morimura Brothers changed their business nature to wholesaling from retailing and had dozens of their affiliated decoration factories all over Japan. **Backstamps 1 through 4** are from that era. The country of origin was marked in Chinese characters on these, not in English. In 1890 the McKinley Tariff Act was passed and beginning in 1891 it became necessary that all the products coming to the United States be stamped. Since that time "Nippon" had appeared as part of the backstamp until "Japan" replaced it in 1921.

Backstamp #5 was registered in Japan in 1919 but the items bearing this backstamp can date back as far as 1891. If the backstamp is green it's an indication of first grade wares, the blue backstamp means second grade.

In 1904 the Noritake factory was founded and called Nippon Kaisha Ltd. (now, Noritake Co., Limited). The company was established at 510 Mukai, Takahamura, Aichi Gun, Aichi Prefecture. "Noritake" took its name from the village of Noritake. The Noritake Co. says in their brochure entitled "History of the Noritake Back Stamp" that

"the trademark which is found on manufactured goods can be called a kind of face of the enterprise which serves society as a guarantee of the quality of the goods, and expresses the responsibility and reliability of the company. Trademarks or brand names which were put on various kinds of porcelain represented the spirit of our founders who pioneered in the manufacture of chinaware. They also symbolized Japanese porcelain which has spread to every part of the world. The trademark of a product is the primary means by which the manufacturer wins the respect of the consumers for the quality and reliability of its products".

Backstamp #6 was registered in Japan in 1908. The RC stands for Royal Crockery (fine china). The symbol design is called "Yajirobe" (toy of balance). It symbolizes the balance in management.

Backstamp #7 is found on items manufactured for the domestic market in Japan. Items bearing this mark date back as early as 1906. The date of registration, however, is unknown. It has the RC for Royal Crockery (fine china) and the symbol design "Yajirobe".

Backstamp #8 was registered in Japan in 1911 although the year of manufacture of items bearing this mark is as early as 1906. The RC stands for Royal Crockery (fine china). Pieces with this backstamp were intended for the domestic market in Japan.

Backstamp #9 is found on items intended for the domestic market in Japan. The RC stands for Royal Crockery (fine china). 1906 is the year they started to use this backstamp and it was registered in Japan in 1911.

Backstamp #10 was used on items being exported to the United States. The first year of manufacture was 1906. The mark was registered both in Japan and the United States in 1911. The RC stands for Royal Crockery (fine china).

Backstamp #11 was used on items intended for export to the United States. The earliest year of manufacture was 1906 but the date of registration is unknown. The centered design of the stamp was taken from Chinese character "Komaru" meaning difficulty. In the export business, the Noritake Co. had to deal with people from foreign lands who thought and acted in a manner somewhat different from which they were accustomed. Since they had to overcome these difficulties, they chose this character and drew a new design. This progressive thinking was representative of the people of the Meiji Era.

Backstamp #12 is most likely a Noritake backstamp although the company cannot be 100% sure. They feel strongly that it appears to be Noritake's. They say that there were wide ranges of the stylization of the character "Komaru" and this is most likely one of them. The backstamp was probably used on items intended for export beginning in 1906-1908.

Backstamp #13 is a variation of #12 and found on pieces in the white and gold pattern. It evidently does not date back further than 1912. *

Backstamp #14 was used on items being exported to the United States. The beginning year of manufacture was 1906 but the registration date is unknown.

Backstamp #15 was used on items intended for export to the United States. The year of manufature began in 1906 but the registration date is unknown.

Backstamp #16 was used on items being exported to the United Kingdom. It was registered in London in 1908 and in 1911 in Japan. Manufacturing began in 1908. The sign of the "komaru" is used, see backstamp #12.

Backstamp #17 is a variation of #16 but includes design number.

Backstamp #18 is similar to #16 and was evidently used on items being exported out of Japan. It probably falls into the same time period.

Backstamp #19 was used on items intended for export to the United States. The year of manufacture began in 1906 and it was registered in Japan in 1911. RC stands for Royal Crockery (fine china).

Backstamp #20 was registered in London in 1908 and manufacture also began the same year. The "komaru" sign is also incorporated into this backstamp, see backstamp #11.

Backstamp #21 was used on items intended for export to the United States. The "M" stands for Morimura and the wreath was designed from the crest of the Morimuras. Manufacturing items with this backstamp began in 1911. This mark was registered both in Japan and the United States in 1911.

Backstamp #22 has the M in the middle which stands for Morimura and the wreath was designed from the crest of the Morimuras. Manufacturing of items with this backstamp began in 1912 but the registration date is unknown.

Backstamp #23 is a variation of #22 but indicates that the piece has been handpainted.

Backstamp #24 is another variaton of #22 and also indicates that this piece was handpainted and in "The Vitry" pattern.

Backstamp #25 is again another variation of #22 and indicates that the piece was handpainted and in the "Sedan" pattern. This particular mark was used on the first dinnerware set manufactured by the Noritake factory in 1914. The registration date is unknown but the pattern number is listed as D1441.

Backstamp #26 is the backstamp used on items sent to India and Southeast Asia. RC stands for Royal Crockery (fine china). The year of manufacture began in 1914 but the mark was not registered in India until 1926. This was the first time that laurel leaves were used with the RC mark.

Backstamp #27 bears the letter M which stands for the Morimuras. The Noritake Co. says that the country of origin "Nippon" was changed in this mark to "Made in Japan" as early as 1918, however, they have no record to show the date it was registered. The Noritake Co. cannot trace whether or not the green ink is older.

Backstamp #28 is a variation of #27 but has the words "US Design Pat. Applied For" added to it.

Backstamp #29 is again a variation of #27 but utilizes Japanese characters in its backstamp.

Backstamp #30 is still another variation of #27 but also gives us the pattern which is "The Vitry", plus Japanese characters and the number "13672."

Backstamp #31 is another variation of #27 but this mark is found on the white and gold pattern items and gives the early pattern number of "16034."

Backstamp #32 is a variation of #27 giving us Japanese characters and the "No. 25920."

Backstamp #33 is another variation of #27 giving us Japanese characters plus "No. 29612."

Backstamp #34 is a variation of #27 giving us more Japanese characters plus "#39556."

Backstamp #35 is again another variation of #27 but it is the mark familiar to collectors as that of being on the white and gold pattern items. It bears Japanese characters and the pattern number of "43061."

Backstamp #36 is another variation of #27 and gives us the pattern name "Amesbury" plus the "US Design Pat. 61231".

Backstamp #37 is a version of #27 but is familiar to collectors as one of the marks found on the Azalea pattern. It includes Japanese characters plus "19322."

Backstamp #38 is similar to #27 but does not include the words "hand painted."

Backstamp #39 is a variation of #38 but also includes the words "US Design Pat. 61235."

Backstamp #40 is a version of #38 but includes the pattern name of "Sheridan."

Backstamp #41 is also a version of #38 and includes the pattern name of "Lancashire" plus the words "US Design Pat. Applied For."

Backstamp #42 is a version of #38 and includes the pattern name of "Daventry" plus "US Design Pat. Applied For".

Backstamp #43 is still another version of #38 and includes the pattern name of "Amarillo" plus "US Design Pat. Applied For."

Backstamp #44 is again another version of #38 and is familiar to collectors as that of the one found on the Modjeska pattern items.

Backstamp #45 is a version of #38 but is the one found on items in the Grasmere pattern, also see Mark #64.

Backstamp #46 is a version of #38 and found with the pattern name of "Roseara" and the words "US Design Pat. Applied For".

Backstamp #47 is a version of #38 and is found on items in the Winona pattern.

Backstamp #48 is a version of #38 and lists the pattern name of Floreal and the words "US Design Patent Applied For."

Backstamp #49 is a version of #38 and is found on pieces decorated with the Howo bird. It bears the number 10733.*

Backstamp #50 is a version of #27 but the words "Made in Japan" have been changed to "Japan".

Backstamp #51 is a version of #50 but the pattern name of "Goldcroft" has been included.

Backstamp #52 is a version of #50 except that the words "hand painted" do not appear.

Backstamp #53 is a variation of mark #12 but has the words "Made in Japan" included. Note the "komaru" sign which is incorporated into the backstamp.

Backstamp #54 is a variation of #53 but no longer says "Nippon" and includes the pattern number found on the white and gold pieces, "No. 16034."*

Backstamp #55 is found on items decorated in the Noritake Howo pattern but the company does not know when the mark was first used or when it was discontinued.

Backstamp #56 is a mark which the company does not know when it was first used or ended, however, this same backstamp appears on other dinner sets all collected from Australia.

Backstamp #57 is found on pieces in the white and gold pattern. Pattern #D175 has been in production since 1912 and it remains a popular pattern all over the world even now. This mark was registered in Japan in 1930 and in the United States in 1950.

Backstamp #58 is a variation of #57 but also includes Japanese characters.

Backstamp #59 was registered in Japan in 1931. The "M" stands for the Morimuras.

Backstamp #60 is a version of #59 but included the pattern name of "Irvington."

Backstamp #61 is a version of #59 but includes the pattern name of "Eltovar" and the words "US Design Pat."

Backstamp #62 is a version of #59 and includes the pattern names of "Ashby" plus the words "US Design Pat. Applied For."

Backstamp #63 is a backstamp for which the company has no information as to when it began and when it ended. It does have the "M" standing for Morimuras in the mark so it has to date before 1953.

Backstamp #64 is a variation of #63 but gives the pattern name of "Grasmere" plus the words "US Design Pat. 76567." The Grasmere items also are found backstamped with #45.

Backstamp #65 bears the "M" standing for the Morimuras. It was registered in Japan in 1933. The familiar M in wreath mark was changed to show laurel leaves with a ribbon on the bottom. This is the basic design of the backstamp used today only the letter N is used.

Backstamp #66 is a version of #65 and found on the Linden pattern items.

Backstamp #67 is also a version of #65 and found on the Linden items but also gives the "US Design Pat. 98217."

Backstamp #68 is a version of #65 and found on items in the Belvoir pattern.

Backstamp #69 is a version of #65 and found on pieces bearing the Berenda pattern, "124632."

Backstamp #70 is also a version of #65 and found on items in the Homeric pattern.

Backstamp #71 is a version of #65 and found on Lynbrook pattern items.

Backstamp #72 is a version of #65 but the words have been changed to "Made in Japan".

Backstamp #73 has the "M" standing for the Morimuras. This mark was registered in Japan in 1933.

Backstamp #74 is a version of #73 but has the words "US Design Pat. Applied For."

Backstamp #75 is a mark familiar to Azalea pattern collectors. This mark was registered in Japan in 1934.

Backstamp #76 is another mark found on the Azalea pieces but has the numbers "252622" added. These items were given as premiums by the Larkin Co. of Buffalo, NY.

Backstamp #77 was registered in Japan in 1934.

Backstamp #78 bears the "M" for the Morimuras and was registered in Japan in 1940.

Backstamp #79 bears the "M" for the Morimuras and is similar to #78 except for the difference in the crown on top.

Backstamp #80 was registered in Japan in 1940. The "komaru" symbol meaning difficulty was incorporated in it. See backstamp #11 for further information about "komaru". Some have referred to this mark as a "spider" but the company indicates that this is false information.

Backstamp #81 was registered in Japan in 1940 and bears the "M" for the Morimuras.

Backstamp #82 was registered in Japan in 1940 and bears the "komaru" mark, see #11. The initials NTK stand for Nippon Toki Kaisha.

Backstamp #83 was registered in Japan in 1941.

Backstamp #84 is that of "Rose China". Immediately after the war the company resumed production of china but for various reasons they could not manufacture the same high quality china that they had made and exported earlier. Since they wanted to keep the Noritake mark for only the highest quality products they temporarily used the Rose China backstamp. Manufacture of these pieces began in 1946 and the mark was registered in Japan in 1950.

Backstamp #85 was registered in Japan in 1949.

Backstamp #86 is a variation of #85.

Backstamp #87 was registered in Japan in 1949 and the United States in 1950. Manufacture of these items began in 1947. This mark was only used for a year and a half and items bearing this backstamp should have been marked "Rose China". The "komaru" symbol is used, see #11. This mark reflects the conditions of the country during the years of the occupation.

Backstamp #88 is a variation of #87.

Backstamp #89 is also a variation of #87.

Backstamp #90 was registered in Japan in 1949.

Backstamp #91 was registered in Japan in 1949. The year of manufacture also began this year. The "M" stands for the Morimuras.

Backstamp #92 was registered in the United States in 1950. Because Noritake is the name of a place, the word could not be officially registered as a trademark. However, because of the consistently high quality of their products, they were finally given permission to register the name.

Backstamp #93 was registered in Japan in 1953 and was the first backstamp used with the letter "N."

Backstamp #94 is the current backstamp and was registered in Japan in 1964. N is taken from their formal name, Nippon Toki.

Backstamp #95 is a variation of #94.

Backstamp #96 was evidently used in 1953 or later as it bears the N in wreath.

Backstamp #97 is a version of # 57 & #58 and is found on today's white and gold dishes.

*Japanese characters drawn are ficticious.

Backstamp #1

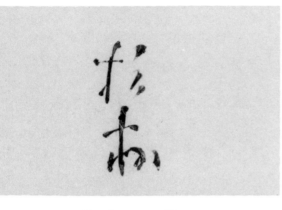

Backstamp #2

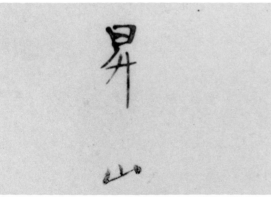

Backstamp #3

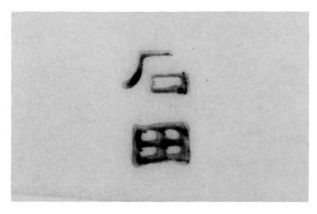

Backstamp #4

Backstamp #5

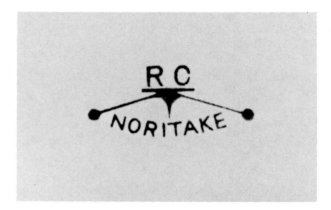

Backstamp #6

Backstamp #7

Backstamp #8

Backstamp #9

No. 16034

Backstamp #13

Backstamp #10

Backstamp #14

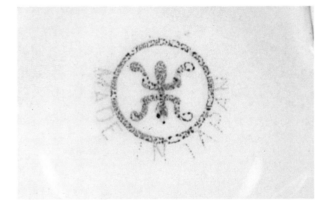

Backstamp #11

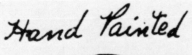

Backstamp #15

Backstamp #12

Backstamp #16

Backstamp #17

Backstamp #21

Backstamp #18

Backstamp #22

Backstamp #19

Backstamp #23

Backstamp #20

Backstamp #24

Backstamp #25

Backstamp #26

Backstamp #27

Backstamp #28

Backstamp #29

Backstamp #30

Backstamp #31

Backstamp #32

Backstamp #33

Backstamp #34

Backstamp #35

Backstamp #36

Backstamp #37

Backstamp #38

Backstamp #39

Backstamp #40

Backstamp #41

Backstamp #42

Backstamp #43

Backstamp #44

Backstamp #45

Backstamp #49

Backstamp #53

Backstamp #46

Backstamp #50

Backstamp #54

Backstamp #47

Backstamp #51

Backstamp #55

Backstamp #48

Backstamp #52

Backstamp #56

Backstamp #57

Backstamp #61

Backstamp #65

Backstamp #58

Backstamp #62

Backstamp #66

Backstamp #59

Backstamp #63

Backstamp #67

Backstamp #60

Backstamp #64

Backstamp #68

Backstamp #69

Backstamp #73

Backstamp #77

Backstamp #70

Backstamp #74

Backstamp #75

Backstamp #78

Backstamp #71

Backstamp #79

Backstamp #72

Backstamp #76

Backstamp #80

Backstamp #81

Backstamp #85

Backstamp #89

Backstamp #82

Backstamp #86

Backstamp #90

Backstamp #83

Noritake

MADE IN
OCCUPIED JAPAN

Backstamp #87

Backstamp #91

Backstamp #84

Backstamp #88

Noritake

Backstamp #93

Backstamp #95

Backstamp #94

Backstamp #96

Backstamp #97

Plate Photos and Descriptions

Plate 1. Three footed bowl (for view of inside see plate 3), 6¾″ wide, green mark #27.

Plate 2. Compote, 9¾″ wide including handles, red mark #27.

Plate 3. Same bowl as Plate 1, but this photo shows artwork inside.

Plate 4. Bowl, 6¼″ wide, green mark #27.

Plate 5. Bowl, 8″ wide, mark #27.

Plate 6. Bowl, 6″ wide, mark #16.

Plate 7. Nappy, 6½″ wide, mark #27.

Plate 8. Bowl, 7″ wide, red mark #27.

Plate 9. Bowl, 11″ wide including handles, green mark #27.

Plate 10. Bowl, 7″ wide, green mark #27.

Plate 11. Bowl, 9¼″ wide, green mark #27.

Plate 12. Bowl, 6½″ wide, green mark #27.

Plate 13. Bowls, each 6½″ wide, green mark #27.

Plate 14. Candy dish, 6″ wide, red mark #27.

Plate 15. Bowl, 6¾″ wide, red mark #27.

Plate 16. Bowl, 5¾″ wide, red mark #27.

Plate 17. Bowl, 7¾″ wide, red mark #27.

Plate 18. Nappy, 5″ in diameter, green mark #27.

Plate 19. Bowl, 7″ wide, green mark #27.

Plate 20. Compote, 11½″ wide, green mark #27.

Plate 21. Bowl, 9½″ wide, red mark #38.

Plate 22. Bowl, 10½″ in diameter, green mark #27.

Plate 23. Bowl, 6″ wide, red mark #27.

Plate 24. Bowl, 8¼″ wide, green mark #27.

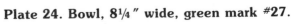

Plate 25. Bowl, 5½" long, green mark #27.

Plate 26. Bowl, 7" wide, green mark #27.

Plate 27. Bowl, 10" wide, green mark #27.

Plate 28. Bowl, 7" wide, green mark #27.

Plate 29. Bowl, 7¼" wide, green mark #27.

Plate 30. Bowl, 8½" wide, green mark #27. Bowl, 8½" wide, green mark #27.

Plate 31. Bowl, 5″ wide, red mark #27.

Plate 32. Bowl, 6¾″ wide, red mark #27. Bowl, 6¾″ wide, green mark #27.

Plate 33. Bowl, 7″ wide, red mark #27.

Plate 34. Bowl, 8¾″ wide, red mark #27.

Plate 35. Bowl, 9¾″ wide, red mark #27.

Plate 36. Compote, 8½″ wide, red mark #27.

Plate 37. Bowl, 6½″ wide, red mark #27.

Plate 38. Bowl, 6¼″ wide, green mark #38.

Plate 39. Bowl, 6½″ in diameter, red mark #27.

Plate 40. Bowl, 8″ wide, green mark #27.

Plate 41. Bowl, 6¼″ wide, red mark #27.

Plate 42. Compote, 9″ wide, mark #27.

111

Plate 43. Syrup, 4½″ tall, green mark #27.

Plate 44. Sauce dish, 4″ tall, red mark #27.

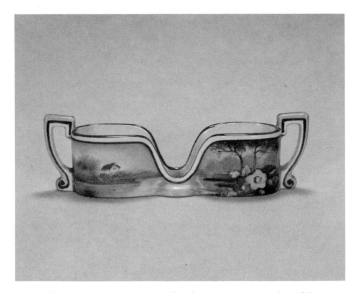

Plate 45. Spooner, 8″ long, red mark #27.

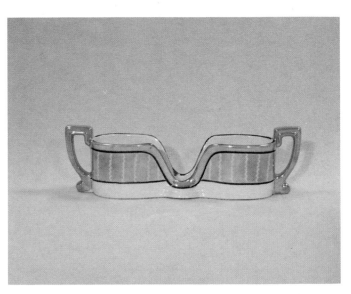

Plate 46. Spooner, 8″ long, red mark #27.

Plate 47. Egg warmer, 5½″ wide, green mark #27. Egg warmer, 5½″ wide, green mark #27.

Plate 48. Syrup, 4½″ tall, green mark #27.

Plate 49. Syrup, 4½″ tall, green mark #27.

Plate 50. Syrup, 4¼″ tall, green mark #27.

Plate 51. Sauce dish, 3¼″ tall, underplate is 6¼″ in diameter, green mark #27.

Plate 52. Mustard jar, 3″ tall, green mark #27.

Plate 53. Mustard jar, 3½″ tall, green mark #27.

Plate 54. Mustard jar, 2½″ tall, green mark #27.

Plate 55. Sauce dish, 5″ wide, red mark #27.

Plate 56. Sauce dish, bowl 3″ tall, underplate 6½″ in diameter, green mark #27.

Plate 57. Sauce dish, underplate is 6¼″ wide, red mark #27.

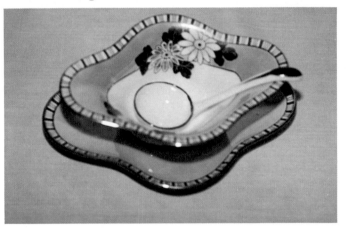

Plate 58. Sauce dish, 6¼″ long, underplate is 7¼″ wide, green mark #27.

Plate 59. Sauce dish, 4½″ in diameter, green mark #27.

Plate 60. Sauce dish, underplate is 5½″ wide, red mark #27. Collectors should note that the term sauce dish is interchangeable with gravy dish, mayonnaise dish or whipped cream dish. This type of item was used for all these purposes.

Plate 61. Sugar bowl, 3½″ tall, red mark #27.

Plate 62. Individual salt, 2-1/8″ wide, mark #16.

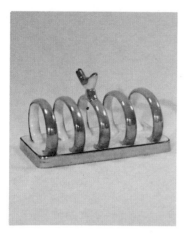

Plate 63. Toast rack with figural bird finial, 5½″ long, green mark #27.

Plate 64. Toast rack, 5½″ long, green mark #27.

Plate 65. Tea tile, 5″ wide, green mark #27.

Plate 66. Lemon dish, 5¾″ wide, red mark #27.

Plate 67. Lemon dish, 5¾″ wide, red mark #27.

Plate 68. Honey jar, 5½″ tall, applied figural bees, green mark #27.

Plate 69. Lemon dish, 6½″ long, red mark #27.

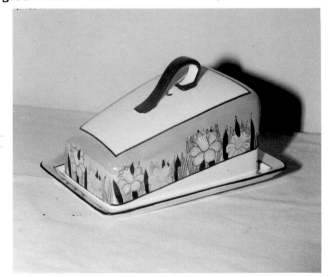

Plate 70. Slanted cheese dish, 8″ x 6″ x 4″, green mark #27.

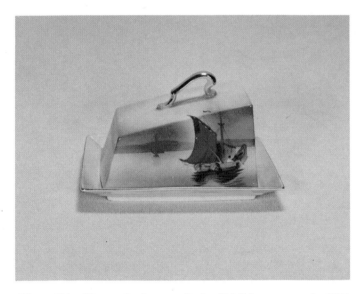

Plate 71. Slanted cheese dish, 6¼″ long, mark #17.

Plate 72. Jam jar, 3½″ tall, red mark #27.

Plate 73. Mustard jar, 2½″ tall, green mark #27.

Plate 74. Mustard jar, 2½″ tall, green mark #27.

Plate 75. Jam jar, 5½" tall, green mark #27.

Plate 76. Mustard jar, 2½" tall, green mark #27.

Plate 77. Sugar shaker, 6½" tall, mark #38.

Plate 78. Creamer, 5¾" tall, red mark #27.

Plate 79. Jam jar, 3½" tall, green mark #27. Jam jar, 4¾" tall, red mark #27.

Plate 80. Tea tile, 6½" wide, red mark #27.

Plate 81. Egg cup, 3½″ tall, green mark #27.

Plate 82. Jam jar, 5″ tall, mark #27.

Plate 83. Jam jar, 5″ tall, mark #27.

Plate 84. Jam jar, 5″ tall, green mark #27.

Plate 85. Jam jar, 5¼″ tall, red mark #27. Jam jar, 5¼″ tall, red mark #27.

Plate 86. Napkin rings, each 2¼″ wide, green mark #27.

Plate 87. Pair of egg cups, 3½″ tall, red mark #27.

Plate 88. Art Deco napkin rings in original box, 2¼″ wide, red mark #27.

118

Plate 89. Art Deco napkin rings in original box, 2¼″ wide, red mark #27.

Plate 90. Egg cup, 2½″ tall, green mark #27. Egg cup, 3½″ tall, red mark #27.

Plate 91. Condiment set, 5½″ wide, red mark #27.

Plate 92. Sugar bowl, same pattern as Plate # 97, 3¼″ tall, green mark #27.

Plate 93. Individual nut cups, green mark #27.

Plate 95. Condiment set, 5½″ wide, red mark #27.

Plate 94. Salt shaker, 2½″ tall, green mark #27.

Plate 96. Condiment set, 7½″ long, red mark #27.

119

Plate 98. Mustard jar, 3¼″ tall, red mark #38. Condiment set, tray is 4¾″ in diameter, red mark #38.

Plate 97. Condiment set, tray is 6¾″ wide, green mark #27.

Plate 99. Open salt and pepper set, tray is 5″ long, green mark #27.

Plate 100. Art Deco sweetmeat set, green mark #27.

Plate 101. Tray, 12″ long, green mark #27.

120

Plate 102. Nappy, 8″ wide, green mark #27.

Plate 103. Tray, 12″ long, blue mark #16.

Plate 104. Coaster, 4″ wide, green mark #27.

Plate 105. Candy dish, 7½″ wide, red mark #27.

Plate 106. Bread and butter set, large dish is 7½″ wide, smaller ones are 3¾″ wide, set comes with six smaller size dishes, all have red mark #27.

Plate 107. Small serving dish. 7¾″ wide, red mark #27.

Plate 108. Bread and butter set, larger dish is 7¼″ wide, six small ones are 3¾″ wide, green mark #27.

Plate 109. Two tier dish, 8¾″ wide, green mark #27.

Plate 110. Chip and dip set, 9¾″ wide, green mark #27.

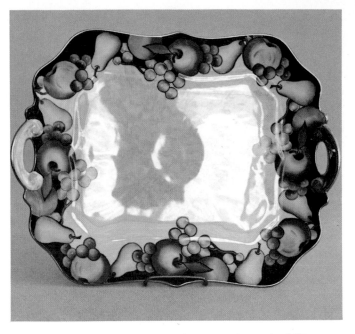

Plate 111. Tray, 11″ long, red mark #27.

Plate 112. Mug, 3¼″ tall, green mark #27. Child's mug, 2½″ tall, green mark #27.

Plate 113. Three handled toothpick, 2¼″ tall, green mark #27.

Plate 114. Condensed milk container, 5¼″ tall, green mark #27.

Plate 115. Shaving mug, 3¾″ tall, green mark #27.

Plate 116. Mustache cup and saucer, saucer is 5¾″ in diameter, green mark #27.

Plate 117. Lemon dish, 6¼″ wide, red mark #27.

Plate 118. Cake plate, 11″ wide, red mark #27.

Plate 119. Small serving dish, 5″ wide, red mark #27.

123

Plate 120. Sandwich plate, 8″ wide, mark #27.

Plate 121. Cake plate, 11″ wide, green mark #27.

Plate 122. Cake plate, 9¾″ wide, red mark #27.

Plate 123. Cake plate, 11″ wide, red mark #27.

Plate 124. Sandwich plate, 9¾″ wide, green mark #27.

Plate 125. Cake plate, 8¼″ wide, green mark #27.

Plate 126. Sandwich plate, 9¾″ wide, green mark #27.

Plate 127. Cookie or cracker jar, 8″ tall, green mark #27.

Plate 128. Covered candy jar, 6½″ tall, red mark #52.

Plate 129. Tea caddy, 3¾″ tall, red mark #27.

Plate 130. Butter dish, has figural bud finial, 6½″ wide, red mark #27.

Plate 131. Candy dish, 6½″ in diameter, red mark #32.

Plate 132. Candy dish, 6½″ in diameter, red mark #50.

Plate 133. Cake dishes, 6½″ in diameter, green mark #27.

Plate 134. Cream and sugar set, sugar bowl is 4¼″ tall, green mark #27.

Plate 135. Ferner, 6″ wide, green mark #27. Ferner, 7″ wide, green mark #27.

Plate 136. Lobster set, underplate is 10¾″ in diameter, red mark #27.

Plate 137. Potpourri jar, 6″ tall, red mark #27.

Plate 139. Sugar and cream set, sugar bowl is 4½ ″ wide, red mark #27.

Plate 138. Sugar and cream set, creamer is 3½ ″ tall, open sugar is 4½ ″ wide, mark #34.

Plate 140. Potpourri jar, 6½ ″ tall, green mark #27.

Plate 141. Wall pocket, 8 ″ long, red mark #38.

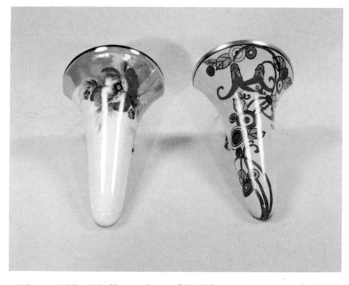

Plate 142. Wall pocket, 8½ ″ long, red mark #27.
Wall pocket, 8¼ ″ long, red mark #29.

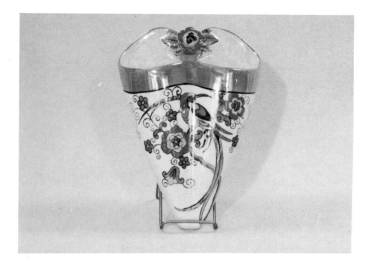

Plate 143. Double wall pocket, 8 ″ long, red mark #27.

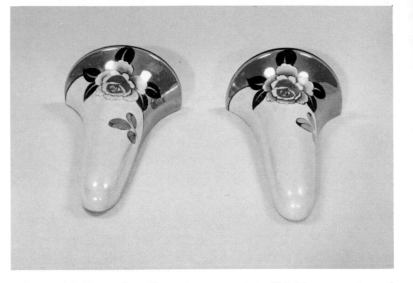

Plate 144. Wall pocket, 8¼″ long, red mark #27.

Plate 145. Pair of wall pockets, each is 8¼″ long, red mark #27.

Plate 146. Wall pocket, 6″ long, red mark #27. Wall pocket, 8½″ long, red mark #33.

Plate 147. Trinket box, 3″ tall, green mark #27.

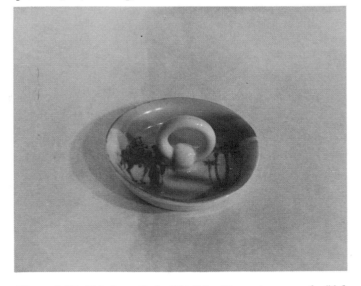

Plate 148. Trinket dish, 2¼″ in diameter, mark #16.

Plate 149. Powder box, 3¾″ wide, green mark #16.

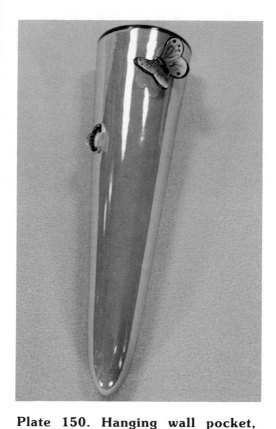

Plate 151. Wall pocket with figural bird applied, 8¼″ long, green mark #27.

Plate 152. Wall pocket, figural butterfly and bee applied, marked "Del Water Gap, Pa.", red mark #27. Wall pocket with figural butterfly and bee applied, 5¼″ long, green mark #27.

Plate 150. Hanging wall pocket, figural butterflies applied, 8¼″ long, red mark #27.

Plate 153. Cologne bottle, 5½″ tall, red mark #27. Cologne bottle, 6″ tall, red mark #27. Cologne bottle, 6¾″ tall, red mark #27.

Plate 154. Wall pocket, 9″ long, red mark #27.

Plate 155. Powder puff box, 4″ wide, green mark #27. Powder puff box, 4″ wide, green mark #27.

Plate 156. Powder puff box, 4″ wide, green mark #27. Powder puff box, 3¾″ wide, green mark #27.

Plate 157. Dresser tray, 13″ long, blue mark #16.

Plate 158. Ring tree, 3″ wide, blue mark #16.

Plate 159. Dresser set, tray is 13″ long and candlesticks are 5¾″ tall, blue mark #16.

Plate 160. Powder puff box, 4″ wide, green mark #27.
Powder puff box, 4″ wide, red mark #27.

Plate 161. Powder puff box, 3″ wide, red mark #27.
Powder puff box, 3¼″ wide, red mark #27.

Plate 162. Dresser set, tray is 12½″ long, candlesticks are 5¼″ tall, blue mark #16.

Plate 163. Wall plaque, 8½″ wide, green mark #27.

Plate 164. Wall plaque, 10″ wide, red mark #27.

Plate 165. Dresser tray, 8¼″ wide, red mark #27. Dresser tray, 6¾″ wide, red mark #27.

Plate 166. Dresser set, tray is 12½″ long, green mark #27.

Plate 167. Powder puff box in Art Deco style with original painted puff, figural flower finial, 3¾″ wide, red mark #27. Powder puff box with figural flower finial, 3¾″ wide, red mark #27.

Plate 168. Desk set with figural flower finials, 6½″ long, red mark #27.

Plate 169. Wall plaque, 6½″ wide, green mark #27.

Plate 170. Wall plaque, 7¾″ wide, red mark #27. Wall plaque, 8¾″ wide, green mark #27. Wall plaque, 5¼″ wide, red mark #27.

Plate 171. Hanging plaque, 10″ wide, mark #7.

Plate 172. Hanging plaque, 7½″ wide, green mark #27.

Plate 173. Hanging plaque, 8½″ wide, green mark #27.Hanging plaque, 8½″ wide, green mark #27.

Plate 174. Hanging plaque, 10″ wide, green mark #27.

Plate 175. Vase, 8½″ tall, green mark #27.

Plate 176. Pair of vases, 7½″ tall, red mark #27.

Plate 177. Pair of vases, 7¼″ tall, green mark #27.

Plate 178. Pair of vases, 7½″ tall, green mark #27.

Plate 179. Pair of vases, 7¼″ tall, green mark #27.

Plate 180. Pair of vases, 10″ tall, green mark #16.

Plate 181. Pair of vases, 9¼″ tall, green mark #16.

Plate 182. Pair of vases (so-called "mirror vases" as the painting is reversed on each), 7½″ tall, mark #16.

Plate 183. Vase, 10½″ tall, green mark #27.

Plate 184. Vase, 9½″ tall, green mark #27.

Plate 185. Vase, 11¼″ tall, green mark #27.

Plate 186. Vase, 6¾″ tall, red mark #27. Vase, 8½″ tall, red mark #27.

Plate 188. Vase, 6″ tall, green mark #27. Vase, 9½″ tall, green mark #27.

Plate 187. Vase, 7″ tall, red mark #27. Vase, 7″ tall, green mark #27. Vase, 7¼″ tall, green mark #27.

135

Plate 189. Vase, 7½″ tall, green mark #27. Vase, 6¼″ tall, green mark #27.

Plate 190. Vase, 6″ tall, mark #16. Ewer, 8″ tall, mark #16.

Plate 191. Vase, 5½″ tall, red mark #27.

Plate 192. Vase, 5″ tall, red mark #27.

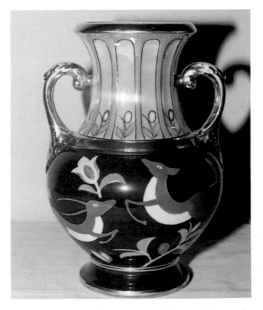

Plate 194. Vase, 6½″ tall, mark #16.

Plate 193. Vase, 10″ tall, mark #16.

Plate 195. Vase, 10″ tall, red mark #27.

Plate 196. Vase, 8¾" tall, green mark #27.

Plate 197. Vase, 8½" tall, mark #16.

Plate 198. Vase, 6¼" tall, green mark #27. Vase, 8½" tall, red mark #33.

Plate 199. Vase, 5¼" tall, red mark #27.

Plate 200. Basket vase, 5½" tall, red mark #27. Basket vase, 7½" tall, red mark #27. Basket vase, 5¾" tall, green mark #27.

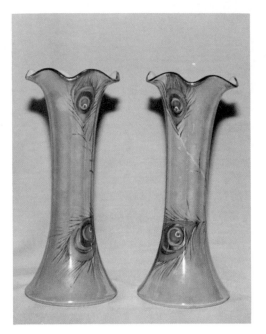

Plate 201. Vase, 8¾″ tall, green mark #27. Vase, 8¾″ tall, green mark #27.

Plate 202. Vase, 7¾″ tall, mark #27.

Plate 203. Pair of vases, each 8″ tall, mark #16.

Plate 204. Vase, 6½″ tall, red mark #27.

Plate 205. Vase, 7½″ tall, red mark #27.

Plate 206. Vase, 6½″ tall, red mark #27.

Plate 207. Candlestick lamps, 5¾″ tall, green mark #27. (One shown before electrical wiring was added.)

Plate 208. Pair of covered urns, 12″ tall, red mark #27.

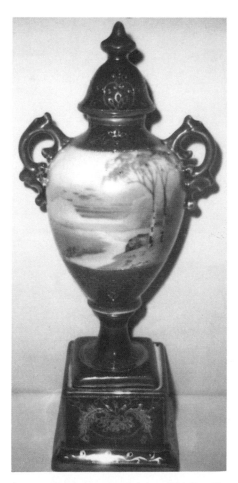

Plate 210. Pair of covered urns, 10¼″ tall, red mark #27.

Plate 209. Covered urn, 8¾″ tall, mark #16.

Plate 211. Lamp, 10″ tall, green mark #27.

Plate 212. Pair of candlesticks, 6½″ tall, green mark #27. Matching bowl, 7½″ in diameter, green mark #27.

Plate 213. Candlestick, 5½″ tall, green mark #27.

Plate 214. Pair of candlesticks, 9″ tall, green mark #27.

Plate 215. Pair of candlesticks, 8¼″ tall, green mark #27.

Plate 216. Pair of candlesticks, 9¼″ tall, green mark #27.

Plate 217. Pair of candlesticks, 7½″ tall, red mark #27.

Plate 218. Pair of candlesticks, 8¼" tall, green mark #27.

Plate 219. Pair of candlesticks, 5½" tall, green mark #27.

Plate 220. Chamberstick, underplate is 4¾" wide, green mark #27.

Plate 221. Mantle set, candlesticks are 3¾" tall, vase is 5¼" tall, red mark #27.

Plate 222. Pair of chambersticks, 6½" tall, green mark #27.

Plate 223. Chamberstick, 4¾″ tall, green mark #27. Chamberstick, 4¾″ tall, green mark #27.

Plate 224. Pair of candlesticks, 3¾″ tall, red mark #27.

Plate 225. Chamberstick, 2¾″ tall, red mark #27. Chamberstick, 1¾″ tall, red mark #27.

Plate 226. Pair of chambersticks, 1¾″ tall, red mark #27.

Plate 227. Pair of chambersticks, 2¼″ tall, red mark #27.

Plate 228. Child's play tea set, tray is 7¼" long and dinner plates are 4¼" wide, red mark #27.

Plate 229. Child's play tea set, teapot is 3½" tall, green mark #27.

Plate 230. Child's play tea set, pot is 3½" tall, green mark #27.

Plate 231. Child's play tea set creamer and sugar, sugar bowl is 2¾″ tall, red mark #27.

Plate 232. Demitasse set, pot is 7¾″ tall, luncheon plates are 7½″ in diameter, sugar bowl is 4½″ tall and the creamer is 3¾″ tall, set comes with six cups and saucers, red mark #27.

Plate 233. Demitasse set, pot is 6¾″ tall, tray is 11¾″ in diameter, set comes with six cups and saucers, red mark #27.

Plate 234. Demitasse set, tray is 12″ wide, pot is 7″ tall, set comes with six cups and saucers, green mark #27.

Plate 235. Chocolate pot, 9″ tall, green mark #27.

Plate 236. Chocolate set, pot is 9″ tall, green mark #27.

Plate 237. Demitasse set, pot is 6¾″ tall, sugar bowl is 4¼″ tall, creamer is 3½″ tall, green mark #27.

Plate 238. Demitasse set, tray is 11¾″ wide, pot is 7″ tall, set comes with six cups and saucers, green mark #27.

Plate 239. Demitasse set, tray is 11¾″ wide, pot is 7″ tall, set comes with six cups and saucers, red mark #27.

Plate 240. Demitasse set, pot is 7″ tall, mark #16.

Plate 241. Chocolate set, pot is 9½″ tall, set comes with four cups and saucers, green mark #27.

Plate 242. Chocolate set, pot is 8¾″ tall, cups are 2¾″ tall, set comes with six cups and saucers, green mark #27.

Plate 243. Chocolate set, pot is 9½″ tall, set comes with six cups and saucers, mark #27.

Plate 244. Chocolate set, pot is 9½″ tall, set comes with five cups and saucers, green mark #27.

Plate 245. Tea set, pot is 6½″ tall, set comes with four cups and saucers, mark #16.

Plate 246. Tea set, pot is 6¾″ tall, sugar bowl is 5½″ tall and the creamer is 5″ tall, set comes with four cups and saucers, mark #16.

Plate 247. Tea set, pot is 5″ tall, luncheon plates are 7½″ wide, sugar bowl is 3¾″ tall, creamer is 2½″ tall, set comes with six cups and saucers and six plates, green mark #27.

Plate 248. Tea set, pot has figural flower bud finials, teapot is 5¾″ tall, luncheon plate is 7¼″ in diameter, set comes with six cups and saucers and six plates, green mark #27.

Plate 249. Tea set, pot is 4¾″ tall, sugar bowl is 4″ tall, creamer is 3¼″ tall, luncheon plates are 7¼″ in diameter, set comes with six cups and saucers and six plates, green mark #27.

Plate 250. Tea set, pot is 4¾″ tall, sugar bowl is 4¼″ tall, creamer is 3¼″ tall, luncheon plates are 7½″ in diameter, set comes with six cups and saucers and six plates, green mark #27.

Plate 251. Tea set, pot is 6″ tall, sugar bowl is 4½″ tall, creamer is 3¼″ tall, green mark #27.

Plate 253. Matching luncheon plate to #251, 7½″ in diameter, green mark #27.

Plate 252. Matching cups, saucers and cake plates to #251, green mark #27.

Plate 254. Snack set, tray is 7½″ long, red mark #27.

152

Plate 255. Tea set, pot is 7″ tall, sugar bowl is 6″ tall, creamer is 4¾″ tall, set comes with six cups and saucers and six plates, red mark #27.

Plate 256. Tea set, pot is 5½″ tall, sugar bowl is 4¼″ tall, creamer is 3¾″ tall, plates are 8½″ in diameter, set comes with six cups, saucers and plates, red mark #27.

Plate 257. Snack set, tray is 8½″ long, red mark #27. Matching creamer and sugar bowl, red mark #27.

Plate 258. Cake set, large plate is 10½″ in diameter, six small plates are 6½″ in diameter, green mark #27.

Plate 259. Fish set, large platter is 16″ long, eight individual serving dishes are 8½″ in diameter, green mark #27.

Plate 260. Game plates, 8″ in diameter, match platter shown in #264, green mark #27.

Plate 261. Game set, 16″ platter, eight plates measure 8½″ in diameter, green mark #27.

Plate 262. Game plate, 8½″ in diameter, red mark #27.

Plate 263. Game plate, 8½″ in diameter, red mark #27.

Plate 264. Game platter, 18″ long, matches plates in #260, green mark #27.

Plate 265. Decanter or cordial set, tray is 8½″ in diameter, decanter is 9½″ tall, individual cordial glasses are 3″ tall, red mark #27.

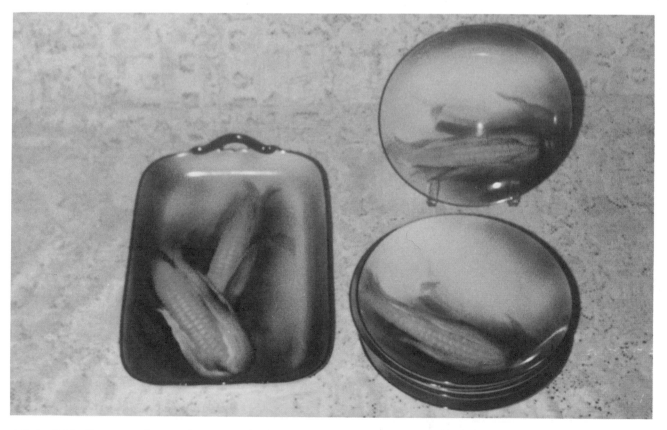

Plate 266. Corn set, large platter is 12″ long and 7¾″ wide, six small plates are 7″ in diameter, green mark #27.

Plate 267. Mantle set, bowl is 9″ wide, candlesticks are 9″ tall, green mark #27.

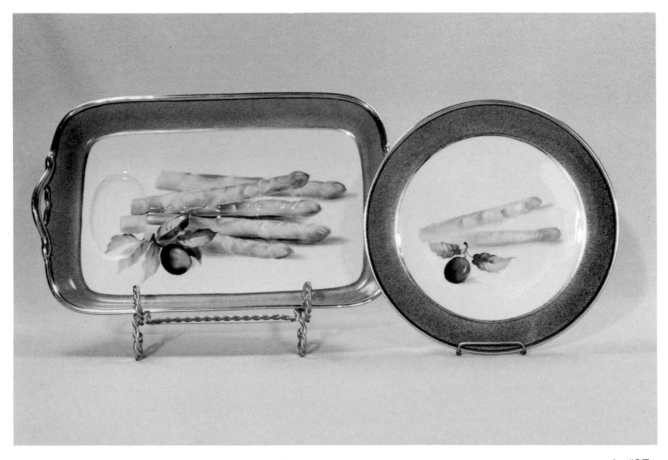

Plate 268. Asparagus set, platter is 11¾″ long, six plates are 7¾″ in diameter, green mark #27.

Plate 269. Celery dish, 11″ long, green mark #27.   **Plate 270. Celery dish, 11″ long, green mark #27.**

Plate 271. Celery dish, 12½″ long, green mark #27.

Plate 272. Luncheon or dessert set, cake plate is 10½″ wide, individual plates are 7″ wide, red mark #27.

Plate 273. Bowl set, large one is 10¾″ wide and six small ones are 6¼″ wide, green mark #27.

Plate 274. Salad bowl, 9¾″ in diameter, red mark #27.

Plate 275. Celery dish, 12″ long, green mark #27.

Plate 276. Celery set, large dish, 12″ long, six salts are 3¾″ long, green mark #27.

Plate 277. Salad set, bowl is 10¼″ wide, six individual plates are 7½″ wide, green mark #27.

Plate 278. Salad bowl, underplate and serving utensils, bowl is 10″ wide, red mark #27.

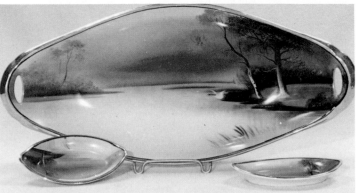

Plate 279. Celery set, large dish is 12″ long, six small salts are 3¾″ long, green mark #27.

Plate 280. Celery set, large dish is 12½″ long, six small salts are 3¾″ long, red mark #27.

Plate 281. Celery set, has figural radishes, large dish is 12½″ long, six small salts are 2¼″ in diameter, green mark #27.

Plate 282. Celery set, large dish is 12¾″ long, six small salts are 3¼″ long, red mark #27.

Plate 283. Celery set, large dish is 13″ long, six small salts are 3½″ long, green mark #27.

Plate 284. Celery set, large dish is 11¾″ long, six salts are 3″ long, green mark #27.

Plate 285. Punch cups, 2¾″ tall, green mark #27.

Plate 286. Cigarette box, 5½″ long, red mark #27.

Plate 287. Pair of ashtrays, 4″ wide, mark #79. Cigarette box, 4¼″ long, mark #79.

Plate 288. Punch set, bowl is 16" wide and 9" tall, eight cups are 2¾" tall, green mark #27.

Plate 289. Punch set, bowl is 13¼" wide, 11¾" tall, eight cups are 2¾" tall, green mark #27.

164

Plate 290. Ashtray, 5¾″ wide, green mark #27.

Plate 291. Ashtray, 3½″ wide, green mark #27.

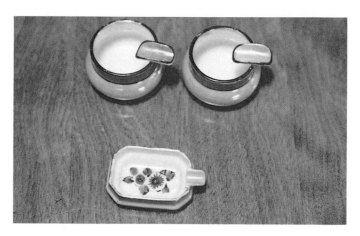

**Plate 292. Ashtrays, 3½″ wide, green mark #27.
Ashtray, 3½″ wide, green mark #27.**

Plate 293. Punch bowl, 16″ wide, green mark #27.

Plate 295. Cigarette box, 5½" long, mark #27.

Plate 296. Cigarette box, 6" long, red mark #27.

Plate 294. Punch bowl, 13½" wide, green mark #27.

Plate 297. Ashtray, 4¼" wide, green mark #27. Ashtray, 5½" wide, green mark #27.

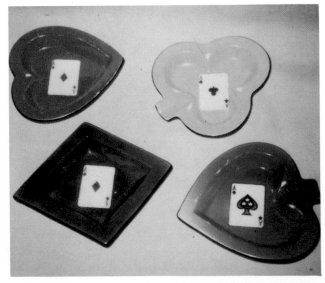

Plate 298. Bridge set ashtrays, note that playing card in red heart has ace of diamonds, green mark #27.

Plate 299. Smoking set, tray is 11½″ long, green mark #27.

Plate 300. Smoking set, tray is 7½″ long, red mark #27.

Plate 301. Smoking set, tray is 11½″ long, green mark #27.

167

Plate 302. Ashtray, 4¼″ wide, shows reverse side of Plate 305, green mark #27.

Plate 303. Ashtray, 5″ wide, green mark #27.

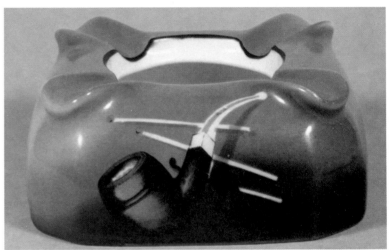

Plate 304. Bridge set, tray is 8¼″ wide, ashtrays are 3¼″ wide, cigarette holder is 3″ tall, this set is same as Plate 307 only it is shown stacked on the tray, red mark #27.

Plate 305. Ashtray, 4½″ square, shows reverse side of Plate 302, green mark #27.

Plate 306. Smoking set, 7¾″ long tray, 3″ tall cigarette holder, green mark #32.

Plate 307. Bridge set, same as Plate 304, red mark #27.

Plate 308. Ashtray, 5″ wide, red mark #27.

Plate 309. Bridge set, ashtrays are in original box, red mark #27.

Plate 310. Smoking set, tray is 7″ long, red mark #27.

Plate 311. Playing card holder (could also be used for cigarettes), 3¾″ tall, red ″ 27. Playing card holder (could also be used for cigarettes), 3¾″ tall, red mark #27.

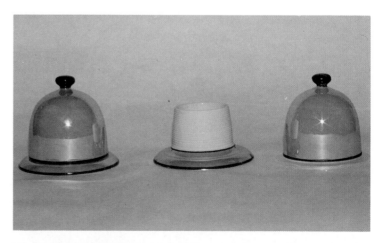

Plate 312. Pair of match holders (notice striking area for match is formed by grooves on side), 3¾″ tall, green mark #27.

Plate 313. Ashtray, 5¼″ wide, green mark #27. Ashtray, 5″ wide, green mark #27.

Plate 314. Ashtray, 5½″ wide, green mark #27.

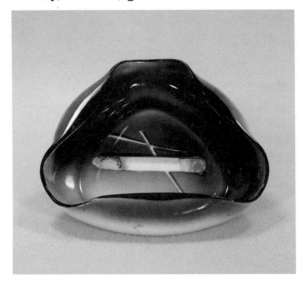

Plate 315. Ashtray, 4½″ wide, green mark #27.

Plate 316. Ashtray, 5½″ wide, green mark #27. Ashtray, 6½″ wide, green mark #27.

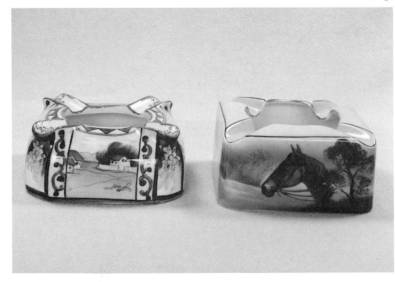

Plate 317. Ashtray, 4″ wide, green mark #27. Ashtray, 4″ wide, red mark #27.

Plate 318. Ashtray, 5″ in diameter, green mark #27.

Plate 319. Ashtray, 4¼″ wide, green mark #27.

Plate 320. Playing card holder (could also be used for cigarettes), 3¾″ tall, green mark #27. Playing card holder (could also be used for cigarettes), 3¾″ tall, red mark #27.

Plate 321. Ashtray, 6¼″ wide, red mark #27.

Plate 322. Cigarette jar (two-piece), 5″ tall, mark #27.

Plate 323. Ashtray, 4¼″ wide, red mark #27. Ashtray, 4¼″ wide, green mark #27.

Plate 324. Bell shaped match holder, 3½″ tall, green mark #27.

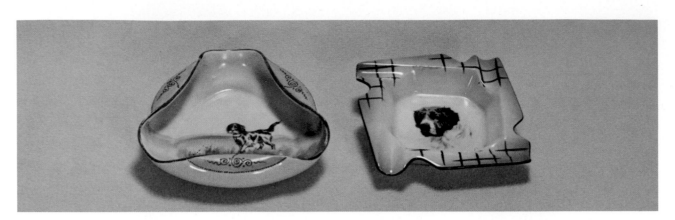

Plate 325. Ashtray, 4¼″ long, green mark #27. Ashtray, 4″ wide, red mark #27.

Plate 326. Match holder, 1¾″ tall, red mark #27. Bell shaped match holder and striker, 3½″ tall, green mark #27.

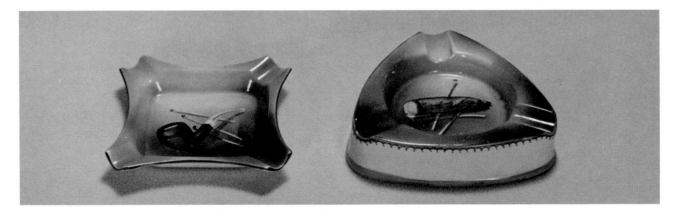

Plate 327. Ashtray, 4½″ wide, green mark #27. Ashtray, 5″ wide, green mark #27.

Plate 328. Hanging match holder, green mark #27. Match holder and ashtray, 3½″ tall, red mark #27.

Plate 330. Humidor, 6½″ tall, green mark #27.

Plate 331. Humidor, 5¾″ tall, green mark #27.

Plate 329. Humidor, 5¾″ tall, green mark #27.

Plate 333. Humidor, 6½″ tall, green mark #27.

Plate 334. Humidor, 5¾″ tall, green mark #27.

Plate 332. Humidor, 6¾″ tall, green mark #27.

Plate 335. Humidor, 5¾″ tall, green mark #27.

Plate 336. Humidor, 5½″ tall, green mark #27.

Plate 337. Humidor, 6″ tall, green mark #27.

Plate 338. Humidors, each 3¾″ tall, green mark #27.

Plate 339. Humidor, 3¾″ tall, green mark #27.

Plate 340. Humidor, 6½″ tall, green mark #27.

Plate 341. Humidor, 5¾″ tall, green mark #27.

174

Plate 342. Humidor, 5½″ tall, green mark #27.

Plate 343. Humidor, 6″ tall, still has original price tag on bottom of $1.98, green mark #27.

Plate 344. Humidor, 4¼″ tall, green mark #27.

Plate 345. Owl night light (also see plate 347), 7½″ tall, green mark #27.

Found on base of ashtray plate 350.

Plate 346. Night light, 9¾″ tall, green mark #27.

Plate 347. Owl night light (see plate 345), 7½″ tall, green mark #27.

Plate 348. Humidors, each 7″ tall, red mark #27.

Plate 349. Night light, 13″ tall to top of bird's head, green mark #27.

Plate 350. Figural ashtray, 5″ wide, writing on bottom says "Hotel McAlpin, New Year's Eve, 1930 red mark #27. Figural ashtray, 6¼″ wide, green mark #27.

Plate 351. Figural ashtray, 5″ wide, green mark #27. Figural ashtray, 5″ wide, green mark #27.

Plate 353. Ashtray with figural bird, 3½″ wide, green mark #27.

Plate 352. Bowl with figural bird, 7½″ long, green mark #38.

Plate 354. Ashtray with figural bird, 4¾″ in diameter, green mark #27.

Plate 355. Figural ashtray, 5¼″ wide, green mark #27.

Plate 356. Nut bowl molded in relief with figural owls on side, 7″ in diameter, green mark #27.

Plate 357. Figural ashtray, 5½″ long, green mark #32.

Plate 358. Figural bowl, 6¾″ long, green mark #27. Figural bowl, 7″ long, red mark #27.

Plate 359. Figural ashtray, 7″ wide, red mark #27. Figural ashtray, 7″ wide, red mark #27.

Plate 360. Figural bird ashtray, 3½″ wide, red mark #27.

177

Plate 361. Bell shaped cigarette holder with figural bird as finial, 5″ tall, green mark #27. Cigarette holder with figural bird as finial, 5″ tall, green mark #27.

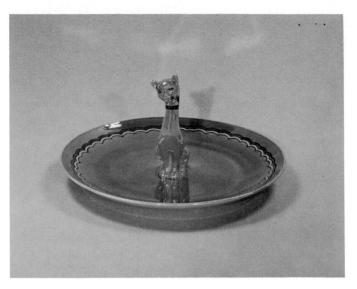

Plate 362. Serving dish with figural cat finial, 8½″ wide, green mark #27.

Plate 363. Cheese and cracker serving dish with figural finial, 9″ wide, green mark #27.

Plate 364. Bell shaped cigarette holder with bird figural finial, 5″ tall, green mark #27. Bell shaped cigarette holder with bird figural finial, 5″ tall, green mark #27.

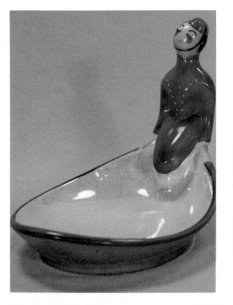

Plate 365. Figural ashtray, 6½″ long, red mark #27.

Plate 366. Figural ashtray, 5¼″ wide, green mark #27. Figural ashtray, 5¼″ wide, red mark #27. Figural ashtray, 5¼″ wide, green mark #27.

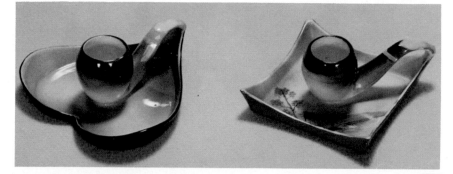

Plate 367. Figural ashtray, 4¾" long, green mark #27. Figural ashtray, 5¼" long, green mark #27.

Plate 368. Bell shaped cigarette holder with bird figural finial, 5" tall, red mark #27.

Plate 369. Powder puff box with figural bird finial, 4" wide, green mark #27. Powder puff box with figural bird finial, 3½" wide, red mark #27.

Plate 370. Napkin ring with figural butterfly sprigged on, 2½" wide, greenmark #27.

Plate 371. Lemon dish with lemon bud finial on edge, 6¾" long, red mark #27.

Plate 372. Figural dresser dolls, all 4½" tall, green mark #27.

179

Plate 373. Figural dresser doll, 5″ tall, red mark #27. Figural dresser doll, 6½″ tall, green mark #32.

Plate 374. Figural dresser doll, 5¾″ tall, green mark #32. Figural dresser doll, 5¾″ tall, green mark #27.

Plate 375. Dresser doll, 5¾″ tall, green mark #32. Clown box, 6″ tall, red mark #32.

Plate 376. Figural inkwells, each 4″ tall, red mark #27.

Plate 377. Figural inkwells, each 3½″ tall, green mark #27.

Plate 378. Figural bell ringer, 3½″ tall, green mark #27.

Plate 379. Figural elephant box, 6½″ tall, red mark #27.

Plate 380. Clown box, 5½″ tall, green mark #27.

Plate 381. Dresser doll, 5½″ tall, green mark #32.

181

Plate 382. Jelly set with figural bee, large dish is 7″ long and six small ones are 2¾″ wide, green mark #27.

Plate 383. Slanted cheese dish with figural bird finial, 7¾″ long, red mark #27.

Plate 384. Figural compote, 7″ tall, red mark #27.

Plate 385. Humidor with figural dog as finial, 5¼″ tall, green mark #27.

Plate 386. Bowl with figural bird inside, 8″ long, green mark #27.

Plate 387. Powder box with figural cat as finial, 4¼″ tall, green mark #27.

Plate 388. Figural inkwell, 4¼″ tall, red mark #27.

Plate 389. Nut dishes with raised nuts and figural squirrel sitting inside of dish, 7½″ long, red mark #27.

Plate 390. Relish dish with figural bird, 8″ wide, green mark #27.

Plate 391. Figural relish set with six individual salts, large dish is 6¾″ long and salts are 2¼″ wide, green mark #27.

Plate 392. Figural swan set (used for candy or nuts), large swan is 7½″ long and small ones are 5″ long, red mark #27.

Plate 393. Figural swan set, large swan is 6″ long, small ones are 2½″ long, red mark #27.

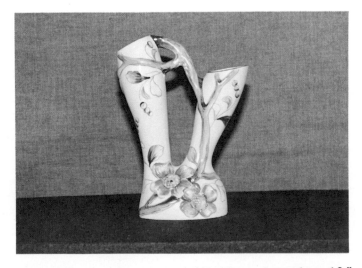

Plate 394. Double vase with figural tree branches, 10″ tall, red mark #27.

Plate 395. Figural vase, 7″ tall, green mark #27.

Plate 396. Figural vase, 7″ tall, green mark #27.

Plate 397. Figural vase, bird and tree trunk, 5¼″ tall, green mark #27.

Plate 398. Figural tulip vase, 5½″ tall, red mark #27.

Plate 399. Figural flower holder, 4¾″ tall, green mark #27.

Plate 400. Figural vase, 5¼″ tall, green mark #27.

Plate 401. Figural flower holder, 4¼″ tall, green mark #27.

Plate 402. Items imitative of Wedgwood's jasper ware. Potpourri jar, 6¾″ tall, red mark #50. Cigarette box, 5½″ long, red mark #50. Vase, 6¾″ tall, red mark #50.

Plate 403. Bowl with heavy silver overlay trim on edge, 10″ long, green mark #27.

Plate 404. Tea set with heavy gold overlay, pot is 5¾″ tall, sugar bowl is 4¾″ tall, creamer is 3¾″ tall, set comes with six cups & saucers, green mark #27.

Plate 405. Pair of vases with heavy gold overlay, 7¼″ tall, mark #16.

Plate 406. Vase imitative of Wedgwood's Jasper ware, 9½″ tall, blue mark #16.

Plate 407. Basket vase with heavy gold overlay, 8¾″ tall, mark #16.

Plate 408. Etched gold serving dish, 7″ long, red mark #27.

Plate 409. Man on camel scene. Pair of vases, 5¾″ tall, mark #16. Serving dish, 9″ long, mark #16.

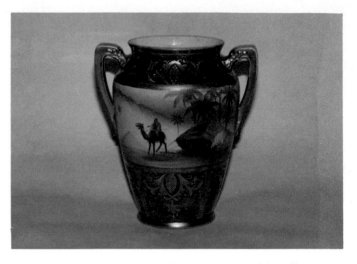

Plate 411. Man on camel scene vase, 8″ tall, green mark #27.

Plate 410. Man on camel scene. Candlestick, 5¼″ tall, mark #16.

Plate 413. Man on camel scene. Cookie or cracker jar, 7″ tall, mark #16.

Plate 412. Man on camel scene. Small punch bowl or fruit compote, 10″ wide, mark #16.

Plate 414. Man on camel scene. Compote, 8½″ wide, 3½″ tall, mark #16.

Plate 415. Man on camel scene. Basket dish, 7½″ long, green mark #27.

Plate 416. Man on camel scene. Squatty vase, 2½″ tall, mark #16.

Plate 417. Man on camel scene. Wall plaques, 8½″ wide, mark #16.

Plate 418. Molded in relief peanut set with six small dishes, large bowl is 6½″ long, small ones are 3″ long, green mark #27.

Plate 419. Molded in relief nut set, large bowl is 6¼″ long, six individual ones are 2″ wide, green mark #27.

Plate 420. Molded in relief peanut set with six small dishes, large bowl is 7″ long and the small ones are 3″ long, green mark #27.

Plate 421. Molded in relief peanut set, large bowl is 7¼″ long and the four small ones are 3″ long, green mark #27.

Plate 422. Molded in relief nut set, large bowl is 6″ long, seven individual size nut cups are 2″ long, green mark #27.

Plate 423. Molded in relief nut bowl, 8¼″ in diameter, green mark #27.

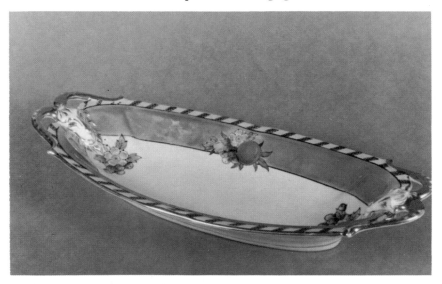

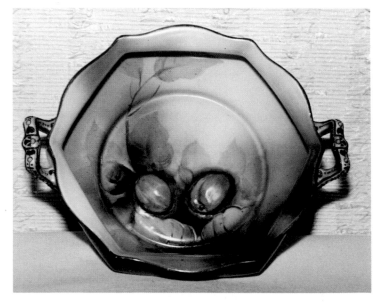

Plate 424. Celery dish with molded in relief goat's heads for handles, 12½″ long, green mark #27.

Plate 425. Lemon dish with lemon molded in relief, 6¼″ wide, red mark #27.

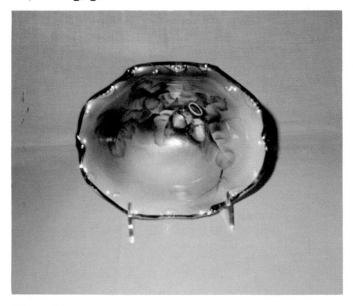

Plate 426. Molded in relief nut dish, silver trim, 8″ long, green mark #27.

Plate 427. Molded in relief nut dish, 8″ wide, green mark #27.

Plate 428. Molded in relief nut bowl with squirrel on front, 6½″ long, green mark #27.

Plate 429. Molded in relief basket, 6″ long, green mark #27.

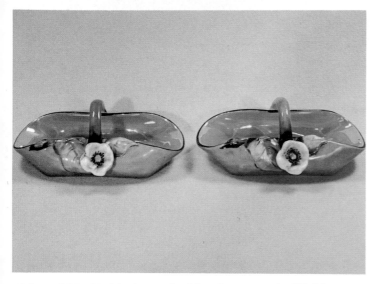

Plate 430. Molded in relief baskets, each 6½″ long, red mark #27.

Plate 431. Molded in relief nut bowl, has silver handle, 7½″ in diameter, green mark #27.

Plate 432. Molded in relief lemon dish, 6″ wide, mark #27.

191

Plate 433. Molded in relief wall plaque, 10½″ wide, green mark #27.

Plate 434. Molded in relief wall plaque, 10½″ wide, green mark #27.

Plate 435. Molded in relief wall plaque, 10½″ wide, green mark #27.

Plate 436. Molded in relief wall plaque, 10½″ wide, green mark #27.

Plate 438. Molded in relief ashtray, 4½″ wide, green mark #27. Molded in relief ashtray, 5½″ wide, green mark #27.

Plate 437. Molded in relief vase, 5¼″ tall, green mark #27.

Plate 439. Molded in relief ashtray, 6″ wide, green mark #27. Molded in relief ashtray, 4¾″ wide, green mark #27.

Plate 440. Bowl with molded in relief ram's heads as handles, 11″ wide, green mark #27.

Plate 441. Molded in relief lemon dish, 6″ wide, red mark #27.

Plate 442. Molded in relief humidor, 7″ tall, green mark #27.

Plate 443. Molded in relief humidor, 6¾″ tall, green mark #27.

Plate 444. Molded in relief humidor, 7″ tall, green mark #27.

Plate 445. Molded in relief humidor, 6¼″ tall, green mark #27.

Plate 446. Molded in relief humidor, lion killing the python, 6¾″ tall, green mark #27.

Plate 447. Molded in relief humidor, 6¼″ tall, green mark #27.

194

Glossary

Art Deco - a style of decoration which hit its peak in Europe and America around 1925 although items were manufactured with this decor as early as 1910. The style was modernistic. Geometric patterns were popular. Motifs used were shapes such as circles, rectangles, cylinders and cones.

Art Nouveau - the name is derived from the French words meaning new art. During the period of 1885-1925 artists tended to use bolder colors and realism was rejected. Free flowing designs were used breaking away from the imitations of the past. Although it lasted until 1925 its popularity waned after 1910.

Azalea pattern - pattern found on both Nippon and Noritake marked items. The pattern is one of pink azaleas with green to gray leaves and gold rims. Nippon era pieces match the later Noritake items. This pattern was exclusive with the Larkin Co. and was offered to its customers as a premium.

Backstamp - mark found on items identifying the manufacturer, exporter or importer and country of origin.

Blank - greenware of bisque items devoid of decoration.

Blown-out - this term is used by collectors and dealers for items that have a relief molded pattern embossed on by the mold in which the item was shaped. It is not acutally "blown-out" as glass items are but the pattern is raised up from the background of the item. See relief molded.

Biscuit - clay which has been fired but unglazed.

Bisque - same as biscuit, term also used by collectors to describe a matte finish on an item.

Casting - the process of making reproductions by pouring slip into molds.

Cha no yu - Japanese tea ceremony.

Chargers - archaic term for large platters or plates.

Cheese hard clay - same as leather hard clay.

Cobalt oxide - blue oxide imported to Japan after 1868 for the decoration of wares. Gosu, a pebble found in Oriental riverbeds had previously been used but was scarce and more expensive than the imported oxide. Cobalt oxide is the most powerful of all the coloring oxides for tinting.

Decalcomania - a process of transferring a wet paper print onto the surface of an item. It was made to resemble hand painted work.

Diaper pattern - repetitive pattern of small design, often geometric or floral.

Dragons (ryu) - a symbol of strength, goodness and good fortune. The Japanese dragon has three claws and was thought to reside in the sky. Clouds, water and lightning often accompany the dragon. The dragon is often portrayed in high relief using the slip trailing method of decoration.

Drain mold - a mold used in making hollow ware. Liquid slip is poured into the mold until the desired thickness of the walls is achieved. The excess clay is then poured out. When the trim starts to shrink away from the mold it is removed.

Drape mold or flopover mold - used to make flat bottomed items. Moist clay is rolled out and draped over the mold. It is then pressed firmly into shape.

Etched gold - engraving by "biting out by acid" on the pieces.

Figural - items having either a relief figure attached for ornamentation to an utilitarian item or the item is a figure that is utilitarian by itself.

Figurine - a small molded figure or statuette with no moving parts. It is strictly ornamental and not utilitarian.

Finial - the top knob on a cover of an item, used to lift the cover off.

Firing - the cooking or baking of clay ware.

Flux - an ingredient added to glaze to assist in making the item fire properly. It causes the glaze to melt at a specified temperature.

Glaze - composed of silica, alumina and flux and is applied to porcelain pieces. During the firing process the glaze joins together with the clay item to form a glasslike surface. It seals the pores and makes them impervious to liquids.

Gold trim - has to be fired at lower temperatures or the gold would sink into the enameled decoration. If overfired the gold becomes discolored.

Greenware - clay which has been molded but not fired.

Hard paste porcelain - paste meaning the body of substance, porcelain being made from clay using kaolin. This produces a hard translucent body when fired.

Howo and Hoo bird - sort of a bird of paradise which resides on earth and is associated with the Empress of Japan. Also see phoenix bird.

Jasper ware - see wedgwood.

Jigger - a machine resembling a potter's wheel. Soft pliable clay is placed onto a convex revolving mold. As the wheel turns, a template is held against it trimming off the excess clay on the outside. The revolving mold shapes the inside of the item and the template cuts the outside.

Jolley - a machine like a jigger only in reverse. The revolving mold is concave and the template forms the inside of the item. The template is lowered inside the revolving mold. The mold forms the outside surface while the template cuts the inside.

Kaolin - a highly refractory clay and one of the principal ingredients used in making porcelain. It is a pure white residual clay.

Kiln - oven in which pottery is fired.

Larkin Co. - founded in Buffalo, N.Y. in 1875. This company imported many items manufactured by the Noritake Co. and sold them through their mail order catalogs.

Leather hard clay - clay which is dry enough to hold its shape but still damp and moist, no longer in a plastic state, also called cheese hard.

Liquid slip - clay in a liquid state.

Luster decoration - a metallic type of coloring decoration giving an iridescent effect.

Matte finish - also referred to as mat and matt. A dull glaze having a low reflectance when fired.

McKinley Tarrif Act of 1890 - Chapter 1244, Section 6, states "That on and after the first day of March, eighteen hundred and ninety one, all articles of foreign manufacture, such as are usually or ordinarily marked, stamped, branded, or labeled, and all packages containing such or other imported articles, shall, respectively, be plainly marked, stamped, branded, or labeled in legible English words, so as to indicate the country of their origin and unless so marked, stamped, branded, or labeled they shall not be admitted to entry".

Molds - contain a cavity in which castings are made. They are generally made from plaster of paris and are used for shaping clay objects. Both liquid and plastic clay may be used. The mold can also be made of clay or rubber, however, plaster was generally used as it absorbed moisture immediately from the clay. Raised ornamentation may also be formed directly in the mold.

Moriage - refers to applied clay (slip) relief decoration. This was usually done by slip trailing or hand rolling and shaping the clay on an item.

Morimura Bros. - importers of Japanese wares in the United States. It was founded in 1876 in Tokyo and a store was opened in NYC in 1877. The NYC store was closed in 1941.

Overglaze decoration - a design is either painted on or a decal applied to an item which already has a fired glazed surface. The article is then refired to make the decoration permanent.

Paulownia flower - crest of the Empress of Japan.

Phoenix bird - sort of a bird of paradise which resides on earth and is associated with the Empress of Japan. This bird appears to be a cross between a peacock, a pheasant and gamecock. There appear to be many designs for this bird. It is also a symbol to the Japanese of all that is beautiful.

Plastic clay - clay in a malleable state, able to be shaped and formed without collapsing.

Porcelain - a mixture composed mainly of kaolin and petuntse which is fired at a high temperature and vitrified.

Potter's wheel - rotating device on which a ball of plastic clay is placed. The wheel is turned and the potter molds the clay with his hands and is capable of producing cylindrical objects.

Press mold - used to make handles, finials, figurines, etc. A two-piece mold into which soft clay is placed. The two pieces are pressed together to form items.

Relief molded - the pattern is embossed on the item by the mold in which the article is shaped. These items give the appearance that the pattern is caused by some type of upward pressure from the underside. Collectors often refer to these items as "blown-out".

Slip - liquid clay.

Slip trailing - a process where liquid clay was applied to porcelain via a rubber tube. It is a form of painting but with clay instead of paint. The slip is often applied quite heavily and gives a thick, raised appearance.

Solid casting mold - used for shallow type items such as bowls and plates. In this type of mold the thickness of the walls is determined by the mold and every piece is formed identically. The mold shapes both the inside and the outside of the piece and the thickness of the walls can be controlled.

Sprigging - the application of small molded relief decoration to the surface of porcelain by use of liquid clay as in Jasper ware.

Sprig mold - a one-piece mold used in making ornaments. Clay is fitted or poured into a mold which is incised with a design. Only one side is molded and the exposed side becomes the back of the finished item.

Taisho - name of period reigned over by Emperor Yoshihito in Japan from 1912-1926. It means great peace.

Ultraviolet lamp - lamp used to detect cracks and hidden repairs on items.

Underglaze decoration - this type of decoration is applied on bisque china (fired once), then the item is glazed and fired again.

Wedgwood - term used to refer to pieces which attempt to imitate Josiah Wedgwood's Jasper ware. The items generally have a light blue or green background. White clay slip was usually trailed onto the background color of the item by use of tubing to form the pattern. The sprigging technique was employed on other pieces.

Yoshihito - Emperor of Japan from 1912-26. He took the name of Taisho which meant great peace.

Index To Items By Plate Numbers

Bibliography

Butler Bros. catalogs, #'s 2177, 2375, 2515, 2558, 2561, 2639, 2651, 2657, 2849, 3062, 4123, 4806

Florence, Gene, *The Collector's Encyclopedia of Occupied Japan Collectibles*, Collector Books, Paducah, KY 1979

Jakeman, Alan, *Getting to Know Japan*, Coward-McCann, Inc., 1960

Kidder, Edward, *Ancient Japan*, The John Day Co., N.Y., 1970

Koyama, Fuijo, *Japanese Ceramics*, Gihodo Printing Co. and Hanshicki Printing Co., Japan, 1961

Larkin catalogs, #'s 75, 78, 86, 89-101, 103-105, 107-124

Reynolds, Robert L., *Commodore Perry In Japan*, American Heritage Publishing Co., Inc., N.Y., 1963

Rundle Scott F., *An Introduction to Japanese History*, International Society for Educational Information Press, Inc., Japan, 1976

Seward, Jack, *The Japanese*, William Morrow & Co., Inc., N.Y., 1972

Van Patten, Joan, *The Collector's Encyclopedia of Nippon Porcelain*, Collector Books, Paducah, KY, 1979

Van Patten, Joan, *The Collector's Encyclopedia of Nippon Porcelain, Series II*, Collector Books, Paducah, KY 1982

Price Guide

The prices printed below are merely a GUIDE and are to be used only as a starting point in arriving at an estimated RETAIL price. Price quotes are given for similar pieces in MINT condition. Adjustments must be made for cracks, chips, worn gold, repairs, etc.

Well-executed pieces are always in demand and their prices continue to rise each year. The increased sophistication and knowledge on the part of today's collector has driven up the prices of the really fine pieces. Because of this, some of the more common items have not risen at all in value and may even have dropped a little in price. Small nut dishes, salt shakers, poorly decorated dinnerware items and similar works will always be flea market material.

There are always collecting trends and the Noritake field is no exception. Art Deco-style pieces seem to have captured the fancy

of many, many collectors and the prices realized for these items reflect it. The patterns are very often geometric, cubist designs. Stylized flowers, butterflies, birds, flappers, elegantly dressed ladies and gentlemen are just a few found. Iridescent finishes and luster glazes were frequently used as well as a number of bold color combinations. Wall pockets, wedgwood-type items, relief molded and figural pieces seem to be very much in demand and low in supply. These items were once low-priced, high quality wares mass produced by the Noritake Company during the 1921-41 manufacturing period. Now their price has adjusted upwards to match their quality.

Collectors should always look for pieces having good workmanship, hand-painted decoration, mint or nearly mint condition and overall quality. This is always a winning combination.

Plate 1.............$40.00–50.00	Plate 53............$25.00–35.00	Plate 104.........$10.00–15.00	2nd Item....$110.00–125.00
Plate 2.............$75.00–100.00	Plate 54............$20.00–30.00	Plate 105.........$25.00–35.00	3rd Item....$175.00–200.00
Plate 3.............$40.00–50.00	Plate 55............$55.00–70.00	Plate 106.........$75.00–85.00 set	Plate 154......$110.00–125.00
Plate 4.............$25.00–35.00	Plate 56............$50.00–65.00	Plate 107.........$35.00–45.00	Plate 155......$150.00–175.00 ea.
Plate 5.............$30.00–45.00	Plate 57............$60.00–75.00	Plate 108.........$75.00–95.00 set	Plate 156......$160.00–185.00 ea.
Plate 6.............$25.00–40.00	Plate 58............$55.00–65.00	Plate 109.........$65.00–75.00	Plate 157.........$50.00–65.00
Plate 7.............$25.00–40.00	Plate 59............$40.00–50.00	Plate 110.........$65.00–75.00	Plate 158.........$40.00–55.00
Plate 8.............$25.00–40.00	Plate 60............$50.00–65.00	Plate 111.........$75.00–95.00	Plate 159......$250.00–275.00
Plate 9.............$85.00–100.00	Plate 61............$15.00–20.00	Plate 112.........$55.00–70.00 ea.	Plate 160......$150.00–175.00 ea.
Plate 10...........$30.00–40.00	Plate 62.............$8.00–10.00	2nd Item........$65.00–75.00	2nd Item....$175.00–195.00
Plate 11...........$55.00–65.00	Plate 63............$80.00–95.00	Plate 113.........$55.00–75.00	Plate 161......$175.00–195.00 ea.
Plate 12...........$35.00–45.00	Plate 64............$60.00–70.00	Plate 114.........$65.00–85.00	2nd Item....$175.00–195.00
Plate 13...........$30.00–45.00 ea.	Plate 65............$30.00–45.00	Plate 115.........$85.00–95.00	Plate 162......$195.00–225.00
Plate 14...........$25.00–40.00	Plate 66............$25.00–30.00	Plate 116.........$75.00–90.00	Plate 163......$215.00–235.00
Plate 15...........$25.00–40.00	Plate 67............$25.00–30.00	Plate 117.........$15.00–20.00	Plate 164......$215.00–235.00
Plate 16...........$25.00–45.00	Plate 68............$60.00–75.00	Plate 118.........$35.00–40.00	Plate 165......$225.00–250.00 ea.
Plate 17...........$25.00–40.00	Plate 69............$25.00–30.00	Plate 119.........$20.00–25.00	2nd Item....$225.00–250.00
Plate 18...........$25.00–40.00	Plate 70............$75.00–85.00	Plate 120.........$40.00–50.00	Plate 166......$195.00–225.00
Plate 19...........$25.00–40.00	Plate 71............$75.00–85.00	Plate 121.........$35.00–40.00	Plate 167......$145.00–160.00
Plate 20...........$70.00–80.00	Plate 72............$25.00–35.00	Plate 122.........$35.00–45.00	2nd Item....$120.00–135.00
Plate 21...........$35.00–45.00	Plate 73............$20.00–30.00	Plate 123.........$35.00–45.00	Plate 168......$200.00–225.00
Plate 22...........$55.00–70.00	Plate 74............$20.00–30.00	Plate 124......$110.00–120.00	Plate 169......$100.00–115.00
Plate 23...........$25.00–40.00	Plate 75............$50.00–65.00	Plate 125.........$35.00–45.00	Plate 170......$195.00–210.00
Plate 24...........$25.00–45.00	Plate 76............$25.00–30.00	Plate 126.........$40.00–50.00	2nd Item....$215.00–230.00
Plate 25...........$25.00–45.00	Plate 77............$25.00–30.00	Plate 127......$100.00–115.00	3rd Item....$195.00–210.00
Plate 26...........$35.00–45.00	Plate 78............$25.00–30.00	Plate 128......$175.00–200.00	Plate 171......$165.00–180.00
Plate 27...........$50.00–65.00	Plate 79............$60.00–75.00 ea.	Plate 129......$200.00–225.00	Plate 172......$145.00–160.00
Plate 28...........$55.00–65.00	2nd Item........$60.00–75.00	Plate 130.........$40.00–55.00	Plate 173......$130.00–145.00 ea.
Plate 29...........$40.00–55.00	Plate 80.........$95.00–105.00	Plate 131......$200.00–225.00	2nd Item....$130.00–145.00
Plate 30...........$40.00–55.00 ea.	Plate 81............$20.00–25.00	Plate 132......$150.00–170.00	Plate 174......$130.00–145.00
2nd Item........$65.00–85.00	Plate 82............$45.00–60.00	Plate 133.........$10.00–15.00 ea.	Plate 175......$100.00–120.00
Plate 31...........$25.00–40.00	Plate 83............$45.00–60.00	Plate 134.........$30.00–35.00	Plate 176......$125.00–140.00 ea.
Plate 32...........$30.00–45.00 ea.	Plate 84............$45.00–60.00	Plate 135.........$85.00–100.00 ea.	Plate 177......$250.00–275.00 pr.
2nd Item........$35.00–45.00	Plate 85............$55.00–70.00	2nd Item......$85.00–100.00	Plate 178......$250.00–275.00 pr.
Plate 33...........$40.00–55.00	2nd Item........$45.00–60.00	Plate 136.......$90.00–115.00	Plate 179......$300.00–325.00 pr.
Plate 34........$125.00–145.00	Plate 86............$35.00–45.00 ea.	Plate 137.........$60.00–75.00	Plate 180......$300.00–325.00 pr.
Plate 35...........$45.00–60.00	Plate 87...........$35.00–40.00 ea.	Plate 138.........$45.00–60.00	Plate 181......$300.00–325.00 pr.
Plate 36...........$45.00–65.00	Plate 88........$125.00–145.00 set	Plate 139.........$30.00–45.00	Plate 182......$300.00–325.00 pr.
Plate 37...........$40.00–60.00	Plate 89........$125.00–145.00 set	Plate 140.........$70.00–85.00	Plate 183......$150.00–175.00
Plate 38...........$40.00–50.00	Plate 90............$35.00–40.00 ea.	Plate 141.........$75.00–85.00	Plate 184......$125.00–140.00
Plate 39...........$30.00–40.00	2nd Item........$35.00–40.00	Plate 142.........$75.00–95.00 ea.	Plate 185......$150.00–175.00
Plate 40...........$35.00–45.00	Plate 91............$75.00–95.00	2nd Item........$75.00–95.00	Plate 186......$200.00–225.00 ea.
Plate 41...........$75.00–85.00	Plate 92............$20.00–30.00	Plate 143......$125.00–135.00	2nd Item....$200.00–225.00
Plate 42...........$45.00–60.00	Plate 93.............$8.00–10.00 ea.	Plate 144......$75.00–85.00	Plate 187.........$75.00–95.00
Plate 43...........$45.00–60.00	Plate 94...............$5.00–8.00	Plate 145.......$75.00–90.00 ea.	2nd Item....$95.00–120.00
Plate 44...........$30.00–45.00	Plate 95............$75.00–95.00	Plate 146......$125.00–145.00	3rd Item......$95.00–125.00
Plate 45...........$35.00–45.00	Plate 96............$65.00–80.00	2nd Item....$165.00–185.00	Plate 188......$55.00–70.00
Plate 46...........$35.00–45.00	Plate 97...........$85.00–105.00	Plate 147......$50.00–65.00	2nd Item....$100.00–125.00
Plate 47...........$85.00–95.00 ea.	Plate 98............$20.00–25.00	Plate 148......$15.00–25.00	Plate 189......$75.00–95.00 ea.
2nd Item........$85.00–95.00	2nd Item........$45.00–50.00	Plate 149......$35.00–45.00	2nd Item....$75.00–95.00
Plate 48...........$50.00–65.00	Plate 99............$55.00–65.00	Plate 150......$80.00–95.00	Plate 190......$145.00–175.00
Plate 49...........$35.00–45.00	Plate 100.........$80.00–95.00	Plate 151......$175.00–195.00	2nd Item....$210.00–235.00
Plate 50...........$50.00–65.00	Plate 101.........$65.00–80.00	Plate 152......$145.00–165.00	Plate 191.........$70.00–85.00
Plate 51...........$70.00–85.00	Plate 102.........$25.00–30.00	2nd Item....$110.00–120.00	Plate 192......$75.00–90.00
Plate 52...........$25.00–35.00	Plate 103.........$55.00–65.00	Plate 153......$110.00–125.00	Plate 193......$190.00–210.00

Plate 194..........$80.00–90.00
Plate 195......$100.00–120.00
Plate 196........$80.00–100.00
Plate 197......$235.00–250.00
Plate 198........$90.00–125.00
2nd Item $185.00–210.00
Plate 199......$170.00–195.00
Plate 200......$110.00–125.00
2nd Item $120.00–135.00
3rd Item $110.00–125.00
Plate 201......$110.00–135.00 ea.
2nd Item $110.00–135.00
Plate 202......$125.00–150.00
Plate 203......$100.00–115.00 ea.
Plate 204........$95.00–105.00
Plate 205......$175.00–200.00
Plate 206........$95.00–105.00
Plate 207..........$75.00–95.00 ea.
Plate 208......$500.00–550.00 pr.
Plate 209......$235.00–275.00
Plate 210......$300.00–350.00 pr.
Plate 211......$110.00–130.00
Plate 212......$110.00–130.00 pr.
2nd Item $45.00–60.00
Plate 213........$55.00–70.00
Plate 214......$155.00–175.00 pr.
Plate 215......$155.00–175.00 pr.
Plate 216......$155.00–175.00 pr.
Plate 217......$155.00–175.00 pr.
Plate 218......$155.00–175.00 pr.
Plate 219......$110.00–130.00 pr.
Plate 220..........$75.00–85.00
Plate 221......$150.00–165.00 set
Plate 222......$140.00–155.00 pr.
Plate 223........$75.00–100.00 ea.
2nd Item $75.00–100.00
Plate 224......$125.00–140.00 pr.
Plate 225..........$60.00–75.00
2nd Item $35.00–50.00
Plate 226..........$60.00–90.00 pr.
Plate 227..........$60.00–90.00 pr.
Plate 228......$200.00–225.00
Plate 229......$250.00–295.00
Plate 230......$200.00–225.00
Plate 231..........$25.00–35.00
Plate 232......$325.00–375.00
Plate 233......$325.00–375.00
Plate 234......$275.00–300.00
Plate 235..........$60.00–70.00
Plate 236........$95.00–110.00
Plate 237......$350.00–375.00
Plate 238......$250.00–295.00
Plate 239......$250.00–295.00
Plate 240......$225.00–250.00
Plate 241......$200.00–225.00
Plate 242......$250.00–295.00
Plate 243......$160.00–195.00
Plate 244......$250.00–295.00
Plate 245......$250.00–295.00
Plate 246......$325.00–350.00
Plate 247......$325.00–375.00
Plate 248......$150.00–175.00
Plate 249......$225.00–250.00
Plate 250......$225.00–250.00
Plate 251......$100.00–125.00
Plate 252..........$35.00–45.00 set
Plate 253..........$15.00–20.00
Plate 254........$55.00–65.00
Plate 255......$325.00–350.00
Plate 256......$350.00–375.00
Plate 257..........$40.00–65.00 ea.
Plate 258......$100.00–120.00

Plate 259......$700.00–800.00 set
Plate 260..........$60.00–75.00 ea.
Plate 261......$700.00–850.00 set
Plate 262..........$75.00–90.00
Plate 263..........$75.00–90.00
Plate 264......$150.00–170.00
Plate 265......$375.00–425.00
Plate 266......$145.00–160.00
Plate 267......$250.00–275.00
Plate 268......$175.00–195.00 set
Plate 269..........$30.00–40.00
Plate 270..........$25.00–40.00
Plate 271..........$25.00–40.00
Plate 272......$115.00–125.00
Plate 273......$110.00–125.00
Plate 274..........$55.00–70.00
Plate 275..........$25.00–40.00
Plate 276........$95.00–115.00
Plate 277......$165.00–185.00
Plate 278......$100.00–120.00
Plate 279........$95.00–115.00
Plate 280........$95.00–115.00
Plate 281........$95.00–115.00
Plate 282........$95.00–115.00
Plate 283........$95.00–115.00
Plate 284........$95.00–115.00
Plate 285..........$25.00–35.00 ea.
Plate 286......$110.00–120.00
Plate 287......$140.00–160.00
Plate 288...$950.00–1,100.00
Plate 289...$850.00–1,000.00
Plate 290..........$30.00–40.00
Plate 291..........$45.00–55.00
Plate 292..........$20.00–25.00 ea.
Plate 293......$450.00–500.00
Plate 294......$450.00–500.00
Plate 295......$110.00–125.00
Plate 296......$110.00–125.00
Plate 297..........$50.00–65.00 ea.
2nd Item $50.00–65.00
Plate 298........$95.00–110.00 set
Plate 299......$375.00–425.00
Plate 300......$375.00–425.00
Plate 301......$350.00–400.00
Plate 302..........$60.00–75.00
Plate 303..........$45.00–60.00
Plate 304......$300.00–350.00
Plate 305..........$60.00–70.00
Plate 306......$275.00–300.00
Plate 307......$300.00–350.00
Plate 308..........$75.00–95.00
Plate 309......$110.00–135.00 set
Plate 310......$135.00–150.00
Plate 311......$110.00–125.00 ea.
2nd Item $110.00–125.00
Plate 312..........$65.00–85.00 ea.
Plate 313......$110.00–125.00
2nd item $75.00–95.00
Plate 314..........$45.00–65.00
Plate 315..........$45.00–65.00
Plate 316......$115.00–135.00 ea.
2nd Item $115.00–135.00
Plate 317..........$55.00–75.00
2nd Item $65.00–85.00
Plate 318..........$65.00–85.00
Plate 319..........$75.00–95.00
Plate 320......$100.00–120.00 ea.
Plate 321..........$45.00–60.00
Plate 322......$100.00–120.00
Plate 323......$110.00–125.00 ea.
Plate 324........$85.00–105.00
Plate 325..........$65.00–85.00 ea.

2nd Item $65.00–85.00
Plate 326..........$75.00–95.00
2nd Item $95.00–110.00
Plate 327..........$55.00–65.00 ea.
2nd Item $55.00–65.00
Plate 328........$95.00–110.00 ea.
2nd Item $95.00–110.00
Plate 329......$275.00–300.00
Plate 330......$275.00–300.00
Plate 331......$275.00–300.00
Plate 332......$375.00–400.00
Plate 333......$375.00–400.00
Plate 334......$275.00–300.00
Plate 335......$125.00–150.00
Plate 336......$275.00–300.00
Plate 337......$175.00–200.00
Plate 338......$130.00–160.00 ea.
Plate 339......$130.00–160.00
Plate 340......$350.00–375.00
Plate 341......$275.00–300.00
Plate 342......$275.00–300.00
Plate 343......$275.00–300.00
Plate 344......$140.00–165.00
Plate 345......$850.00–950.00
Plate 346...$950.00–1,100.00
Plate 347......$850.00–950.00
Plate 348......$550.00–650.00 ea.
Plate 349......$850.00–950.00
Plate 350......$235.00–260.00 ea.
2nd Item $235.00–260.00
Plate 351......$235.00–260.00 ea.
2nd Item $235.00–260.00
Plate 352........$90.00–110.00
Plate 353........$90.00–110.00
Plate 354......$135.00–150.00
Plate 355......$250.00–275.00
Plate 356......$150.00–175.00
Plate 357......$250.00–270.00
Plate 358........$95.00–115.00 ea.
2nd Item $95.00–115.00
Plate 359......$260.00–295.00 ea.
2nd Item $260.00–295.00
Plate 360........$85.00–100.00
Plate 361......$160.00–175.00
2nd Item $125.00–140.00
Plate 362......$125.00–140.00
Plate 363......$195.00–225.00
Plate 364......$125.00–150.00 ea.
2nd Item $125.00–150.00
Plate 365......$250.00–275.00
Plate 366......$115.00–130.00 ea.
2nd Item $115.00–130.00
3rd Item $115.00–130.00
Plate 367......$115.00–130.00 ea.
2nd Item $115.00–130.00
Plate 368......$115.00–130.00
Plate 369......$145.00–160.00 ea.
2nd Item $145.00–160.00
Plate 370........$45.00–65.00
Plate 371..........$75.00–95.00
Plate 372......$275.00–300.00 ea.
Plate 373......$275.00–300.00 ea.
2nd Item ...$275.00–300.00
Plate 374......$275.00–300.00 ea.
2nd Item $275.00–300.00
Plate 375......$275.00–300.00 ea.
2nd Item $275.00–300.00
Plate 376......$275.00–300.00 ea.
Plate 377......$225.00–240.00 ea.
Plate 378......$275.00–300.00
Plate 379......$225.00–250.00
Plate 380......$275.00–300.00

Plate 381......$275.00–300.00
Plate 382......$100.00–115.00
Plate 383......$115.00–135.00
Plate 384......$295.00–325.00
Plate 385......$300.00–350.00
Plate 386........$95.00–110.00
Plate 387......$175.00–200.00
Plate 388......$110.00–130.00
Plate 389......$115.00–130.00 ea.
Plate 390......$110.00–125.00
Plate 391......$135.00–150.00 set
Plate 392......$135.00–150.00 set
Plate 393......$135.00–150.00 set
Plate 394......$125.00–145.00
Plate 395......$250.00–275.00
Plate 396......$250.00–275.00
Plate 397......$200.00–225.00
Plate 398......$150.00–175.00
Plate 399......$150.00–175.00
Plate 400......$140.00–165.00
Plate 401......$135.00–155.00
Plate 402......$200.00–225.00 ea.
2nd Item $200.00–225.00
3rd Item $200.00–225.00
Plate 403..........$75.00–95.00
Plate 404......$375.00–400.00 set
Plate 405......$300.00–325.00 pr.
Plate 406......$300.00–350.00
Plate 407......$175.00–210.00
Plate 408......$50.00–75.00
Plate 409......$220.00–245.00 pr.
2nd Item $140.00–175.00
Plate 410......$150.00–175.00
Plate 411......$135.00–150.00
Plate 412......$225.00–250.00
Plate 413......$225.00–250.00
Plate 414......$165.00–180.00
Plate 415......$165.00–180.00
Plate 416........$95.00–125.00
Plate 417......$135.00–160.00 ea.
Plate 418......$165.00–185.00
Plate 419......$165.00–185.00
Plate 420......$165.00–185.00
Plate 421......$165.00–185.00
Plate 422......$165.00–185.00
Plate 423......$115.00–130.00
Plate 424..........$55.00–70.00
Plate 425..........$35.00–40.00
Plate 426..........$65.00–85.00
Plate 427..........$65.00–85.00
Plate 428......$125.00–150.00
Plate 429........$85.00–115.00
Plate 430..........$65.00–75.00 ea.
Plate 431......$125.00–140.00
Plate 432..........$45.00–65.00
Plate 433......$600.00–700.00
Plate 434......$550.00–600.00
Plate 435......$450.00–500.00
Plate 436......$600.00–700.00
Plate 437......$150.00–175.00
Plate 438......$150.00–175.00 ea.
2nd item $150.00–175.00
Plate 439......$175.00–200.00 ea.
Plate 440......$145.00–160.00
Plate 441..........$40.00–60.00
Plate 442......$450.00–525.00
Plate 443......$550.00–600.00
Plate 444......$475.00–525.00
Plate 445......$475.00–525.00
Plate 446......$525.00–575.00
Plate 447......$550.00–600.00

Schroeder's ANTIQUES Price Guide

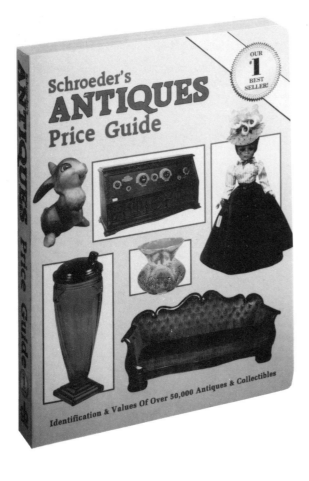

Schroeder's Antiques Price Guide is the #1 best-selling antiques & collectibles value guide on the market today, and here's why . . . More than 300 authors, well-known dealers, and top-notch collectors work together with our editors to bring you accurate information regarding pricing and identification. More than 45,000 items in almost 500 categories are listed along with hundreds of sharp original photos that illustrate not only the rare and unusual, but the common, popular collectibles as well. Each large close-up shot shows important details clearly. Every subject is represented with histories and background information, a feature not found in any of our competitors' publications. Our editors keep abreast of newly-developing trends, often adding several new categories a year as the need arises. If it merits the interest of today's collector, you'll find it in Schroeder's. And you can feel confident that the information we publish is up to date and accurate. Our advisors thoroughly check each category to spot inconsistencies, listings that may not be entirely reflective of market dealings, and lines too vague to be of merit. Only the best of the lot remains for publication. Without doubt, you'll find Schroeder's Antiques Price Guide the only one to buy for reliable information and values.

8½ x 11", 608 Pages   **$12.95**

cb
COLLECTOR BOOKS
A Division of Schroeder Publishing Co., Inc.